The Pyramid
of
Personal
Power

The Pyramid
of
Personal
Power

REACHING NEW HEIGHTS
BY MASTERING
THE FOUR TOOLS
OF DISCIPLINE

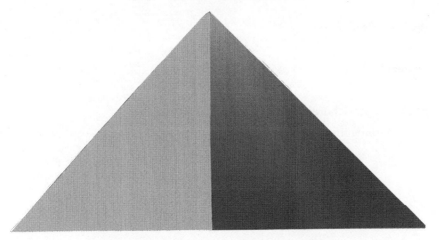

David H. Dupuy

DHD PUBLISHING

The Pyramid of Personal Power

Published by:
DHD Publishing
3020 Canton View Walk
Marietta, GA 30068
davidhdupuy@gmail.com

ISBN:978-0615634487

Printed in the United States of America

Book Design: Deborah Perdue, Illumination Graphics,
www.illuminationgraphics.com

Table of Contents

DEDICATION

To my patient and loving wife, Kim –

I am grateful

for her support and inspiration.

INTRODUCTION

We live in a society with conflicting goals, pressures, and responsibilities that conspire to obscure the magical journey of life. Rather than being responsible for and fully engaged in life, we find ourselves just trying to get by or make do. Although we have a gut feeling we are missing something, we can't quite put our finger on what it is. The obstacles we encounter have a way of wearing us down and making us feel powerless.

Take heart! We don't need to feel powerless! This book provides a framework and a set of tools for effective living. These tools don't necessarily make the challenges easier, but they do prepare us to make *conscious* decisions that affect the trajectory of our lives.

The Economy as an Indicator of the Problem

Although some economists say the Great Recession that began in 2008 is over, its effects will be felt for years to come. You would be hard pressed to find anyone not impacted by the struggles and challenges brought on by the bursting of the mortgage bubble and subsequent financial crisis. The jobless rate remains high and many believe the recovery will be different from those in the past. The days of refinancing our homes at higher valuations and lower rates while pulling out equity for our next car or vacation are gone.

1

I believe the financial crisis was the symptom of a much larger problem. Over the last decade we became a nation that believed the rules of the American Dream had changed. As a nation and as individuals, we lived well beyond our means and built our dreams on the sands of greed and consumerism rather than the bedrock of sound principles.

Despite the formidable challenges that lie ahead, I'm optimistic. I believe each of us recognizes that success only comes as a result of focused effort, correct priorities, and a willingness to objectively assess our skills and abilities. Once we make the commitment to live in sync with guiding principles and values, we have the power to change the trajectory of our lives. Material wants and desires will always be a part of the American Dream, but they must be subjugated to the tools of discipline, not to the whims of emotion.

Noted psychiatrist, author, and speaker M. Scott Peck published *The Road Less Traveled* in 1978.[1] I've read this book many times and it's had a profound impact on my life's journey. Depending on my life stage at the time of each reading, different parts of the book took on higher meaning. For example, the section on Grace meant much more to me as a father of two than it did when I first read the book as a sixteen-year-old student. Dr. Peck had a unique ability to take his scientific and empirical findings and distill them into a form that novices like me could understand and relate to. His books were wildly successful because the truths revealed about behavior, life experience, and spirituality resonated with millions of people struggling to make their way on the "road less traveled."

The Road Less Traveled is must reading. The title alludes to Dr. Peck's calling and encouragement to us all to become more conscious and responsible for our lives. Each of us has the opportunity to read

[1] M. Scott Peck, *The Road Less Traveled* (New York: Simon and Schuster, 1978).

and heed Dr. Peck's advice. We must not allow the influence of society to determine our path in life; instead, we should make our own way. But how do we do that? How do we shape our lives to be in sync with our guiding principles?

In a word, *discipline*.

Dr. Peck defines discipline as "the tools that allow us to solve life's problems."[2] These tools are:

- delayed gratification
- assumption of responsibility
- dedication to the truth
- balance

A defining characteristic of being human is the ability to discipline oneself. When the tools of discipline are used together as described in this book, they release a power that is synergistic and exponential. Each of us is on a journey of discovery in which the tools of discipline are needed to take the next step of personal development in our quest for self-actualization. For most of us, however, the journey to the summit of self-mastery and balance isn't linear. We encounter obstacles along the path and suffer from an imperfect ability to apply these tools of discipline. The purpose of this book is to make us more aware of these powerful tools and to offer advice on how to use them in our lives. As we do so, we'll become more fulfilled and at peace with who we are and what we do.

Let's begin by taking a closer look at how the tools build upon themselves from the fundamental to the advanced—The Pyramid of Personal Power.

[2] Ibid

Unlocking the Power of the Pyramid

The Great Pyramids of Giza were constructed more than 4,000 years ago and are the oldest of the Seven Wonders of the World. Historians debate a number of things about these pyramids, including the technology used to move, cut, and arrange the stones; where the stones were quarried; and who ultimately assembled them. Given the stones' size and weight (up to seventy tons) the pyramids remain an awe-inspiring archeological marvel.

As recently as 1400 AD, the Great Pyramids were the tallest man-made objects on earth. Although more pyramids are found in Egypt than anywhere else (138 and counting), they were constructed as monuments on nearly every continent, with notable examples in Greece, Mexico, China, and India. In all cases, pyramids seem to hold a prominent role in the religious and spiritual development of the respective cultures who built them. They seem to represent man's attempt at connection with the Creator.

Although most archeologists agree that the Great Pyramids were built as tombs for pharaohs, their symbolism and deeper meaning continue to be a mystery. I believe the pyramid represents man's quest for enlightenment as well as his spiritual connectivity with the Creator. For the purposes of this book, the journey up the pyramid represents the climb we're all making toward that capstone of enlightenment. In keeping with this theme, this book arranges the tools of discipline from the more fundamental levels to the more advanced as we move toward the top.

As we move upward, we build on each discipline until we reach the capstone dealing with balance and spirituality. When we operate in balance, we're operating at the highest level as human beings in the material and spiritual worlds.

These steps or blocks represent the tools we use in our journey of self-discovery and creativity. The tools are arranged with each block building on the lower ones. For example, the tool of delayed gratification is at the foundation and must be mastered before we can effectively move on to personal responsibility. Just as the grandest pyramids of Egypt were built from the ground up, we must begin with the foundation. At each step upward, we develop a better or more complete understanding of who we are, what is important to us, and how we can live in a way that more effectively reveals our special gifts.

The first chapter of this book is about *discovery*. Self-discovery is an implicit goal at each step up the pyramid (and in this book). It does not take place at a single place and time. Rather, discovery takes place throughout our lives as we learn new and important facets of who we are and how we're interconnected with those around us. The learning never ends; it merely evolves as we travel up the pyramid. It's vital we become aware that we're on a journey of self-discovery and face many external and internal obstacles along the way. This awareness is the first step in clearing a path of meaningful self-discovery.

Next, the book focuses on the blocks in the pyramid. These represent the *tools of self-discipline* that allow us to enjoy a higher and more rewarding view of who we really are. The higher we climb, the clearer our perspective will be on the world below (our lives, our dreams, our interactions with others). We'll learn that using the tools of delayed gratification, personal responsibility, dedication to the truth, and balance is the ultimate act of love for ourselves and others as we move to the summit. Love is only revealed through the actions we're willing to take on our behalf or for someone else. This journey isn't easy; it requires a great deal of effort. To make these tools more accessible, I dedicate a chapter to each, exemplifying how it reveals itself in our everyday lives.

The first step of the pyramid is the principle of *delayed gratification*. Delayed gratification is best revealed in our daily lives through our material desires and our use or misuse of debt. Next, the principle of *personal responsibility* is revealed in how we handle stress while maintaining a sense of humor in the "pursuit of happiness." Indeed, our happiness is completely up to us and isn't dependent on others.

Dedication to the truth is best revealed in how we give back to society. Striving to make the world a better place moves us from a love of self to a love of others. Giving is living at a higher level, allowing us to appreciate our own blessings by becoming a blessing to others. Finally, we explore the elusive nature of balance and the spiritual necessity of living a balanced life. Quieting the Judging Mind and allowing time for peace and reflection is vital for continued renewal. Balance allows us to be open to the spiritual mysteries of life and to solve problems that cannot be solved by self-effort alone.

Balance is at the summit of the pyramid, and I find it difficult to stay there for long—the oxygen is a bit thin up there. The goal, of course, is to spend more and more time at the summit, balancing the demands of life in a calm, peaceful way. Living a balanced life means becoming more spiritual in our approach to life, less dependent on the material world for fulfillment, and more open to change. We recognize that life is full of changes and we become more accepting of them.

I close the book with a chapter on *creativity*. At its core, creativity is self-change. Most of us find creativity to be exciting and gratifying, even though a bit scary. Creativity is the spice of life that reveals who we are and what we love. Rather than being repelled by forced change, we embrace the change of becoming a creator. Since we're made in the image of our Creator, in order to lead fulfilling lives, we must become creators too. This is the only way to fulfill our destiny. At its best, creativity reveals to us our gifts and special purpose in life. It's depicted as a circle because creativity has no beginning or end; we continually reinvent ourselves throughout life.

As we move through the tools of discipline and unlock the power of the pyramid, it's important to remember that they are only the means to an end—living a life of awareness and being in sync with our special gifts and guiding principles. To that end, I will uncover immutable truths that represent important guideposts for living. Immutable truths are universal laws just like those found in physics or mathematics. When we follow these laws, we find ourselves in harmony with the universe. When we fight against these laws, as many of us do, we find that daily living is very difficult indeed.

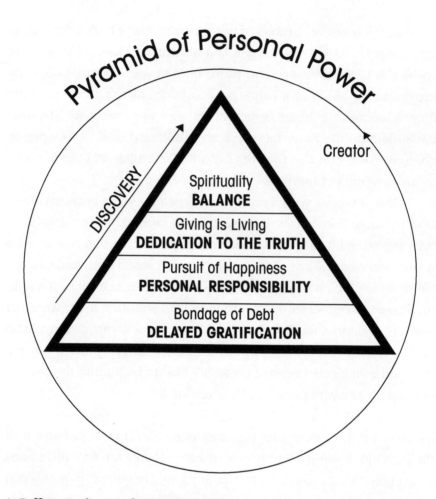

A Call to Action and Awareness

Most of us travel along the path of life *unconsciously*. We may be vaguely aware that a decision here or a choice there contributes to our current situation, but most of us are just living day-to-day either unable or unwilling to connect the dots between our actions and their impact. Our first inclination to negative events may be to say, "Why me? Why is my luck so bad?" Rarely are we able to see clearly how the cumulative effects of our decisions impact our journeys. Rather than blaming others and feeling powerless, using the tools and methods described in this book will allow us to see our own special gifts and strengths and learn how to take more control over our lives.

Perhaps the greatest barrier to taking these first steps toward change is our own inertia. Although life is short, I've found it's just long enough to put off until tomorrow what would best be done today. We're all guilty of procrastination from time to time, but I passionately believe it's vital that we use the ideas and tools presented in this book today, not tomorrow, or we will likely never get around to it.

"Tools" is an important descriptor because an intellectual under-standing of what they are and how they can impact your life is only the first step. Knowing what a hammer is used for is very different from actually using one. The only way to complete a building project is to use the right tools. The "project" in this case is you, and the key to using these tools effectively is to use them every day. It's how you will become conscious of who you are and of the journey you are on.

We all must find a spark of motivation to start using these tools today rather than tomorrow. The habit of tomorrow is a fantasy because nothing ever gets done tomorrow; things only get done today.

I have an idea on how to break away from the pull of inertia into a state of action. I've used this method to achieve excellent results, including the writing and publishing of this book. If you're willing to try it yourself, I think you will find it just as motivating.

I live in a suburb in Northwest Atlanta named Marietta. My family and I really like our little corner of suburbia and have called it home for ten years now. We recently purchased a new "dream house" in Marietta. It's about a half-mile from a fitness center where my wife, Kim, and I work out. I've developed the habit of running or walking to the gym to exercise. Although this habit began as my rather anemic attempt at environmental consciousness, it's had one other valuable side benefit for me. My route takes me past the H. M. Patterson and

Son Funeral Home. It's a rather nice property tucked into the woods adjacent to the historic Brown Cemetery.

Despite its rather idyllic setting, I find the building foreboding and final—it is, after all, a funeral home. Dead people are brought here to receive their final send-off from friends and family. I often think of those who have passed away when I see the parking lot full for another funeral. Did he die in peace? What were her regrets, if any?

The H. M. Patterson and Son Funeral Home reminds me of my own mortality and makes me aware of the relatively short time I have to make a difference in this life and I make a habit of reflecting on various goals every time I pass it. These goals are very important to me, but tend to be non urgent in nature. We all take our health and our independence for granted until they are gone, but no one wants to think about the possibility of illness or the inevitability of death. Yet consider your mortality in light of your own personal goals and how accomplishing these goals will make the rest of your life more fulfilling. Now think about how important it is to begin today rather than tomorrow.

I've had many reasons—excuses—over the last two years to put this book on the back burner. My parents went through a lengthy divorce that required considerable involvement from my two sisters and me. I started a new job that resulted in new challenges, long hours, and significant travel. Then there are the numerous other distractions of everyday life including kids' sports and school activities, house guests, weddings—the list goes on. Many days I felt tired and unmotivated, but passing the funeral home on my way to the gym provided that spark for me.

You don't have to see "my" funeral home, but you should pay attention to the funeral home you pass every day. It's there, on the way to someplace you regularly go. Once you make an effort to notice it, you may find a spark of inspiration to act. If this imagery doesn't work for you, pick something else as a catalyst—remembering a parent or grandparent who passed away with a promising, yet unfulfilled life, or being a good example for your children.

Whatever you choose, find a spark. Making the effort to change will be the most difficult, but ultimately most rewarding gift you can give yourself and your loved ones.

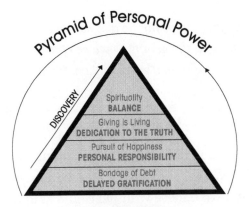

CHAPTER 1

DISCOVERY

"The greatest discovery of any generation is that a human being can alter his life by altering his attitude."
– William James

The Eagle and the Chicken

Once upon a time, a farmer was walking his property when he happened upon a large egg in a field near his farm. The man placed the egg with a clutch of eggs tended to by a barnyard hen, and the eggs eventually hatched into a group of chicks. The large egg was that of an eagle, but the eagle saw himself as a chicken. Raised by the hen, he did as the other chickens, pecking at the ground for seed, insects and worms. He clucked and cackled and would occasionally thrash his wings and fly a few feet in the air—just as the other chickens did.

Years passed and the eagle grew old. One day he saw a magnificent bird flying majestically in the cloudless sky. It glided with grace and majesty among the currents of the wind with barely a flap of its strong, golden wings. The old eagle looked up in awe, "Who's that?" he asked.

"That's the eagle, king of the birds," said his neighbor. "He belongs to the sky. We belong to the ground—we're chickens."

So the eagle lived and died as a chicken, for that is what he thought he was.

–Author Unknown

We are the sum of our beliefs and expectations. If we believe we're chickens, then we'll be chickens regardless of our gifts and capabilities. But if we believe with heart and soul that we're unique creations of God, which each of us is, we'll achieve far more than we ever thought possible.

Most of us are eagles trapped in chicken fears and expectations. We're our own worst critics, highlighting our shortcomings and predicting our failures. How many of us spend time in front of the mirror looking for things to criticize? *My hair is too thin; I don't like my freckles; my ears stick out; I wish my eyes were blue.* And as harsh as we are on our outward appearance, we are often more critical toward our inward attributes: *I'm too shy; I'm not smart enough; I'll never measure up; my dad doesn't love me; my mom doesn't understand me.* When we stop and listen to our Judging Mind, we realize just how damaging negative self-talk and criticism is to our self-image.

Where does this negativity come from? It comes from the insecurities of our egos.

Merriam-Webster's Collegiate Dictionary defines ego as, "the self, especially as compared to another self or the world." Our ego constantly compares itself to the egos or the "self" of others in an effort to protect or enhance our sense of self. Many times, however, our egos move from protection or enhancement mode into attack mode, either attacking our own self or others.

Corrosive self-talk and the ego's negative feelings are often transferred to others in the form of anger, put-downs, or criticism. The subconscious pattern is to push others down in order to pull ourselves up. It's as if the only way we can feel okay about ourselves is to talk about the failings of others. But as Jesus points out in Matthew 12:34 (NIV), "out of the overflow of the heart the mouth speaks." The more negative we are inwardly, the more negative and unhappy we are outwardly. It's vital that we break the cycle of inward negativity and its outward expression that is so damaging, not only to ourselves but to our family, friends, and coworkers.

So is the ego completely bad? Are we doomed to be enslaved to the insecurities of our egos? No. In the book *Egonomics*, David Marcum and Steven Smith explore the role of ego at work and its impact on our lives. Although their focus is on how the egos of individuals and corporations can impact a company's bottom line, their takeaways are relevant to our discussion.

First, they assert that ego is what provides the confidence and ambition necessary to take advantage of our talents and traits[3]. As such, the ego is the engine that drives us to create, to improve, and to take risks in order to achieve our personal goals. Seen in this light, the ego is quite valuable to us and is necessary for growth and development. However, the ego has a dark side and Marcum and Smith emphasize that it must be balanced or our strengths can quickly become our ultimate blind spots:

> The point here is not simply that we all have strengths and weaknesses: "I can see the big picture, but I'm not very good with details," or "I'm good with numbers, but I'm uncomfortable with people." That's typical. The crucial point is that when ego isn't balanced (with what we'll discuss in depth later), it turns our strengths not into polar opposites but into close

---

[3] David Marcum and Steven Smith, *Egonomics* (New York: Simon and Schuster, 2008), 58.

counterfeits. That subtle modification becomes the ultimate blind spot, because our weaknesses feel almost the same to us as our strengths. While the difference isn't discernible to us, it is clear to others. When we spot those weaknesses in ourselves or the work culture we're in, we can be confident negative ego is the culprit.[4]

Our goal is to explore a process that can be used to unlock the treasure within through discovery our unique gifts and strengths while being aware of the potentially negative effects of the ego. This involves five steps:

1. **Quiet the judging ego:** Learn a new paradigm of coaching through experiential learning and awareness.
2. **Take a strength inventory:** Think about those hobbies, situations, or studies that truly absorb your thinking with an effortless focus.
3. **Become aware of shortcomings:** Our greatest strengths can become our greatest weaknesses without self-awareness.
4. **Trust our natural selves:** Trust in self is the cornerstone of a positive self-image and allows for trust in others.
5. **Ongoing self-awareness and management:** We'll explore ways in which to develop habits of self-management that conquer insecurity and self-doubt.

Self-aware versus Self-conscious

Each of us comes from a unique set of circumstances, families, and ethnic backgrounds that impact our life view. It's vital that we become conscious of the views that society, friends, and family place upon us,

Ibid, 34.

as they can become as heavy as a fifty-pound backpack. Unfortunately, it isn't full of necessities and it often becomes an impediment to our journey. It's weighted down with our life's baggage: failures, fears, and insecurities. The key is to limit the amount we take along and the best way to do this is to become conscious of how our minds work and where this baggage comes from. Once we become aware of what is happening, we're in a better position to change our way of thinking and to become more open to the wonderful journey up the pyramid.

Growing up, my father changed jobs frequently. I was born in Philadelphia, but I lived in fourteen houses in ten different cities before I left for college. Being the new kid in town was not easy. I'm a shy person and I just wanted to blend into my new surroundings. Unfortunately (or so I thought), I had two characteristics that made me stand out. First, I was tall and skinny—I want to say slim (ego protection), but I was just plain skinny. Second, my last name is Dupuy. Can you pronounce that? You need some college French classes to get close. (In case you haven't taken French, it's pronounced due-pwee.)

As the new kid, I would often slump down, not wanting to draw attention to myself. But new kids in school always get attention and I was sure my new classmates could see my insecurity. I dreaded roll call when my name inevitably was called, or more appropriately butchered: "David ... Doopey?" "David...Du-prey?" "David ummm, Dopey." Ah, yes, a personal favorite that always got a good laugh from the class. Over time, the slump in my shoulders became permanent. My mom would constantly remind me to sit up straight; she couldn't understand what was wrong with me. This slumping posture was a manifestation of my slumping self-confidence. Over time, I began to withdrawal, which further eroded my self-image.

The numerous family moves only compounded the problem. I remember feeling like a plant that had been transplanted one too many times—shallow roots never allowed time for meaningful growth. I wasn't comfortable with myself. I was incredibly self-conscious of my name, my height, and by fourth grade, my glasses. Self-consciousness stunts growth. It encourages withdrawal and lack of confidence. When you couple self-consciousness with harsh and judgmental input from yourself and others, a positive self-image is nearly impossible.

I suspect I'm not alone in experiencing the world self-consciously. I am fortunate that I had very positive and supporting parents who built me up even when I was trying to tear myself down. Their positive talk helped carry me through some very difficult years. If it wasn't for them, I would have struggled even more mightily through days of negative self-talk and despair. Many people hide these feelings of insecurity and self-consciousness under the varnish of "personality." Whether this personality varnish is calm and cool or bravado and exterior confidence, most people experience a sense of insecurity and a strong desire to fit in socially. Why? What drives this behavior?

Quiet the Judging Ego

It all gets back to the ego or Judging Mind and our deep-seated desire to feel accepted by, or even better for the ego, superior to those around us. Of course, these feelings are complete phantoms of the Judging Mind. Our egos are so fragile that we're constantly attempting to protect ourselves or put down others in order to feel good.

We'll never be able to change how the insecurities and self-consciousness of others may become manifested in put-downs and negativity toward us; however, we have the ability to control our own minds and allow our true nature to shine through. The key to successful self-discovery is to be self-aware while not becoming self-conscious or judgmental. Understanding the difference between the two is vital to successful self-discovery.

When we're self-aware, we observe, in a nonjudgmental fashion, who we are, what we enjoy, as well as our natural strengths and weakness. Alternatively, self-consciousness is the *judgmental* aware-ness of these things and the self-condemnation that often arises from these realizations. The subtle difference between self-awareness and self-consciousness has a huge impact on how we view ourselves, our gifts and our strengths.

In his landmark book *The Inner Game of Tennis*, Tim Gallwey described self-awareness and self-consciousness within the framework of a Self 1 and Self 2 level of consciousness on the tennis court.[5] Self 1 is the ego or Judging Mind that criticizes us when we miss an easy shot or compliments us for making a good serve. Self 2, or what he refers to as the Natural Self, is the self that actually coordinates all the muscles, footwork, and racket positioning to make the shot.

Self 1 is the judge while Self 2 is the doer. Although written for the aspiring tennis player, this book provides an excellent glimpse into human behavior both on and off the court. Think about your own experience in sports where you made a mistake. Did your Self 1 condemn you for your mistake? If you were hard on yourself, did you find that on your next shot you were more nervous? Did your muscles get tighter? Were you afraid of making another mistake? That is the impact your Judging Self has on your Natural Self.

In most cases, our Judging Mind produces the opposite of its intended effect, which is hardly surprising. When someone harshly criticizes us, our Natural Self becomes self-conscious and afraid to make a mistake. But more often than not, this creates a condition of tightness and insecurity that makes mistakes even more likely. So, you might ask, what if we begin praising all the good shots and ignoring

[5] W. Timothy Gallwey, *The Inner Game of Tennis: The Classic Guide to the Mental Side of Peak Performance* (New York, Random House: 1997). Gallwey's work has been adapted far beyond the tennis court to business and personal relationships. I have a personal connection with his original work as a tennis player myself, but the reader may find his other adaptations even more applicable, such as The Inner Game of Business and others in his series.

the bad ones? That doesn't work either, because praise, though better than condemnation, is still judgmental in its derivation. Gallwey points out that praise is only the flipside of the same coin that the Judging Self uses to manipulate the Natural Self. The Natural Self believes it's just one mistake away from harsh condemnation.

The Natural Self is extremely talented. It's able to coordinate multiple functions of the body in order to hit a serve, shoot a basket, or kick a soccer ball. The same is true for all our natural talents or interests in life. The key is to allow the Natural Self, or "the genius within," to learn without interference from the Judging Mind. Think about the best coaches or mentors you had growing up. These coaches asked questions and focused on the results while not making judgments about the person or process.

Our goal is to become our own nonjudgmental coach using awareness and visualization for teaching rather than labels of "good" or "bad." We'll explore the concept of "experiential learning" in more detail later, as it's the only way in which the Natural Self learns. But before that, it's important to see what happens when we operate exclusively within the ego or Judging Mind.

The Judging Mind is the scolding parent, coach, or teacher you may have had growing up. The Judging Mind is quick to blame our Natural Self whenever a perceived error or misstep is detected. Our Natural Self becomes afraid of mistakes and, consequently, freezes, retreats, or otherwise reacts self-consciously. When we're this hard on ourselves, it's not surprising that we're critical of each other. Our harsh self-criticism is projected on friends and loved ones, further impacting our Natural Self when we're on the receiving end of criticism. And so it continues, passed down from parent to child and then on to the playground, classroom, and workplace, reaffirming our insecurities. It's vital that we break this cycle before it diminishes our self-concept and stunts our growth.

IMMUTABLE LAW 1

Our Natural Self is our true self, and we are responsible, through self-discovery, to uncover and live in accordance with our Natural Self.

Here is the crucial point and a cornerstone for self-discovery: the Natural Self is at the core of who we are and it's our job to uncover and live in accordance with our Natural Self. As we grow older, it's almost always obscured to some degree by the conflicting goals of parents, friends, and society as a whole. We go to college, or not, based largely on the opinions and choices of friends and family. Our college major is often picked based on what our parents did, rather than our own interests. How many multi-generational doctors, lawyers, and accountants are there?

In many cases, our jobs choose us due to our family's status, economic conditions, schools, and a perceived lack of control over our options. As we grow older, we become more attuned to listening to the Judging Mind and rarely listen to our Natural Self. But it's still there.

Despite being covered up by years of neglect, our Natural Self remains. It's often experienced as intuition or a gut feeling. When we ignore our intuition, we're ignoring our Natural Self. We should pay attention to our feelings and instincts, and listen to our hearts. Our Natural Self wants us to live in harmony with our strengths and natural gifts.

Useful Tools

After years of listening exclusively to our Judging Minds, we need to rediscover living in accordance with our Natural Self. Here are a few tools we can use to become more connected to our Natural Self:

1. Awareness: We must become aware of the internal dialogue that goes on in our heads. Awareness is the first step toward control of the Judging Mind. Once we become aware of the internal dialogue or what the Judging Self is saying to the Natural Self, we should ask the following questions. Are the comments condemning? What seems to be the common themes of these discussions? Awareness of our self-talk gives us a glimpse of how the Judging Mind works. Our goal is to change our Judging Mind into the "Enlightened Self."

An Enlightened Self is our favorite coach, teacher, or mentor that observes more than judges. Objectively observing what works and what doesn't allows our Natural Self to perform without fear of condemnation. For example, if your job requires that you make multiple cold calls and you find you're nervous on the phone, try this approach. Observe what makes you nervous—usually fear of rejection or failure. Acknowledge that fear, but recognize it as an emotion without any basis in reality. Think about how you speak with a friend or family member and imagine using the same conversational style during your cold call. Are you more or less successful? Track your results and become an objective observer of success rate. Again, the goal is to nurture awareness without the condemnation of failure.

2. Silence through meditation: I know of no better way to quiet the mind than to meditate. We'll discuss later the specifics around how, when, and where to meditate, but for now, think of meditation as a discipline used to silence the mind and its incessant internal dialogue. Meditation is an important tool in gaining control of the Judging Mind, while opening yourself up to the Natural Self.

3. Become your own coach: It's important to differentiate positive coaching from positive self-talk. Positive self-talk is a valuable tool for building self-esteem, or "psyching ourselves up" before a big event, but it has limitations in its ability to truly improve our effectiveness. By positive coaching, I mean a fundamental shift in our approach to learning. Rather than recreating the parent/child relationship, we become an objective observer of our "mistakes."

When we take emotion and condemnation out of the equation, it's amazing how quickly we can improve. The Natural Self becomes more confident and less concerned with failure, which allows for the flow of experiential learning. One of the fundamental truths we'll explore more fully revolves around this truth: "The less concerned we are with failure, the better chance we have in becoming successful in whatever we do."

4. Visualization: The Natural Self learns best when it's allowed to observe others. As a life-long student of tennis, I love to watch the big tournaments such as Wimbledon and the U.S. Open. Whenever I played tennis right after watching these tournaments, my level of play would go up. Then it would go back down and I wondered why. I soon realized it was my Judging Mind showing up and interfering with the visualization that the Natural Self relied on for improvement.

Utilizing these practical tools will begin a metamorphosis of change. It may be slow at first, but with time and consistent practice of these methods, we'll become more calm and balanced. Quieting the Judging Mind allows the true self to shine through. With this new frame of mind or consciousness, we can begin to look at our unique strengths and gifts in a nonjudgmental way.

Setting aside judgment is crucial in this process because an honest appraisal of gifts is the only way we can begin the process of self-actualization. With our coaching mindset firmly in place, we can ask the following questions: What are my strengths? What would my parents say are my unique gifts? What hobbies, events, work, and play do I most enjoy? When am I most happy, focused, or "in the flow" of the moment?

Strength and Gift Inventory

It's impossible to take a strength and gift inventory without asking our friends and family to participate in the exercise. However, our friends and family will often want to categorize our strengths within their subjective framework of good or bad, useful or not useful. In addition, they will often take the leap into suggesting how our strengths and gifts should determine our schooling, vocation, and hobbies. Not only is it completely unnecessary to take this leap, it's damaging in that it constricts our process of discovery.

At this point, we're doing nothing more than asking ourselves, our friends, and family to recall moments in our lives when we were at our best. The terms "in the flow" or "in the zone" are often used to describe the feeling we have when we're completely focused or absorbed in an activity. These situations often provide a glimpse into our core strengths and gifts.

Think back on a time when you were really happy with yourself. What were you doing? Think about people who really mean a lot to you and a recent compliment they paid you. What was it about? When are you most contented? Can you remember studying something in school in which you were completely absorbed? These questions can help you become aware of your strengths and help remind you of your gifts.

Taking a strength inventory is quite simple. You will want at least three other people to participate in the exercise with you—close friends, mentors, family members. On a piece of paper or a spreadsheet, ask them to label "Core Strength" on the left side and "Situation When Used" on the right side. It's important to include the situation as it will help you recall the circumstances and remember the activity and the feelings you had at the time. Finally, ask them to come up with at least three core strengths. Here's an example:

Core Strength	Situation When Used
Relationship builder	PTA committee for school fundraiser
Empathetic listener	When my friend's mother had to go to hospice
Good negotiator	Helping Jim buy his truck and save $500 from what he negotiated
Calm in stressful situations	When our neighbor fell and broke her hip

You must complete your own list prior to receiving feedback from others. Now that you have at least four different lists, it's time to take inventory of your strengths. Most people will find recurring themes in the strengths highlighted by others. These recurring themes give you a glimpse into your unique gifts. Ultimately, you will want to refine, improve, and build up those gifts in order to maximize your effectiveness and enjoyment of life.

We're much happier and at peace when we're utilizing our strengths and unique gifts. Remember, a self-conscious person only focuses on weaknesses, whereas a self-aware person knows her weaknesses but balances that knowledge with a keen focus of her strengths.

Building Up Our Unique Gifts

There is no question that Michael Jordan and Mia Hamm have unique athletic gifts, but where would they be without significant focus on those gifts? Without focus and practice utilizing our core strengths, they languish and never reach full potential. The realization of our unique gifts isn't enough; we must put forth effort to realize the fruit of these gifts in our lives.

In order to build self-confidence, we must take an inventory of strengths, and no matter how undeveloped we may consider them, work diligently to grow those acorns into oak trees. Building up our strengths builds our confidence and self-image. Just as a house will fall if its foundation isn't sound, our ability to develop good relationships as well as work with and trust others is based exclusively on our personal foundation and belief in ourselves. Remember, it starts with us.

IMMUTABLE LAW 2
Unless we proactively utilize our core strengths,
we will never be in a position to realize our unique potential.

So, how do we begin the process of improving and refining our unique gifts? In a word, we must be proactive.

Being proactive is a habit of action and personal responsibility. It's the recognition that personal evolution does not begin externally but internally. By being proactive, we take our list of core strengths and begin to systematically integrate them into our everyday life. Tiger Woods may be a gifted athlete, but without practice, he would never reach his potential. So it is with each of us; without using our gifts daily we'll only realize a small fraction of our incredible potential.

Once we take our strength inventory, we must share it with people we trust completely—a parent, spouse, or mentor. Get their feedback, then add to or refine the inventory. Once we have these qualities, strengths, and gifts firmly in mind, it's best to work systematically on each one using the following process:

1. Track on your calendar: Most everyone utilizes a calendar; however, it often includes only the basics of appointments or task lists.

It's vital that you expand your calendar to incorporate working on strengths or you will not remember to do so. Highlight one strength at the beginning of each month—that is the key strength you will focus on for the month. Whether you use a view per month, week or day, the strength you're working on should be highlighted and readily available.

2. Incorporate activities that exercise this strength into your daily routine: As part of your daily, weekly, and monthly checklists of "to dos," incorporate the strength of the month. For example, I might incorporate a meeting with a client in which we plan to show specific financing or acquisition alternatives. The goal isn't only to understand how these ideas might add value to the client's core business, but to also better understand the challenges confronting the client's business. Our follow-up meeting might be focused on how to solve a problem based on this initial meeting. By exercising my relationship strength, I'm giving myself multiple opportunities to engage the client. Over time, these experiences will yield new business.

3. Month-end evaluation: Review and assess how you did. Did you listen effectively? Were there takeaway ideas that you need to make sure you follow up on? Are you looking at the situation from the others' perspective; seeking ways to help them? Monthly self-evaluation is crucial, as it allows you to reaffirm your strength before moving on to the next focus.

Franklin's Example

This process is remarkably similar to a process described by Benjamin Franklin in his autobiography. As all students of history know, Franklin was a man of many talents: inventor, writer, orator, diplomat, and successful business owner. What many may not know is that his great genius may never have become fully appreciated without his great personal effort to build up his strengths and minimize his weaknesses.

But one of his greatest strengths, his intellect, became one of his greatest weaknesses early on in his political career. His intelligence resulted in a lack of patience with those he did not feel had reasonable business or political acumen. In fact, he was very confrontational in his disagreements with others. His skill as a communicator and orator meant he often won arguments and made others look foolish in the process. What he learned over time, however, was that although he won many arguments, he was shut out from potential business and political opportunities due to his perceived arrogance and combative style. He realized that, in order to capitalize on his personal gifts, he had to change his style. He went on to utilize a version of the approach described above to become more amiable and less of a threat to the establishment.

The lesson here is to not be arrogant about our strengths, but to build them up in a harmonious, constructive way to be more confident in ourselves while maintaining an awareness of our limitations. Always remember that our greatest strengths tend to be our greatest weaknesses.

Our greatest strength is often our greatest weakness.

Being self-aware isn't being self-conscious; instead, it's utilizing our strengths in a way that maximizes our ability to be effective. Celebrating our strengths while being aware of our weaknesses will keep us grounded and ultimately enhance our success. The chart below takes the strengths discussed earlier and highlights the potential ego risk or weaknesses associated with the core strength. It's important to take this final step in our strength inventory in order to become aware of the pitfalls of the ego.

Core Strength	Ego Risk
Relationship builder	Politically motivated
Empathetic listener	Too easily swayed: pushover
Good negotiator	Win-lose mentality
Calm in stressful situations	Dispassionate, remote

Visualize to Actualize

In addition to incorporating strengths into our daily lives, visualization techniques will reinforce our desired behaviors. It's important for the purposes of strength building to understand how vital it is to use visualization in conjunction with experience to facilitate growth and confidence. When you were taking your strength inventory, I asked you to recall a moment when you were performing at a high level. What were you doing? How did it feel? You are using visualization to recall those events. Visualization uses your imagination to take your experience to the next level.

Visualization allows you to take a strength and use it over and over again in various mental vignettes to reaffirm that core ability. The visualization can either be a memory of past successes, or it can be a totally imagined situation where you utilize your strength to achieve a personal goal. We all have the capacity to take a visualized image and replay it over and over again in our minds to create an experience.

Using the "Relationship Builder" strength as an example, let's imagine I want to utilize that strength with a business prospect. He represents a very important business opportunity, but I haven't met this client, nor do I understand the issues present in his business. I do, however, know how I have interacted with countless clients to more fully appreciate their business situations. I sit quietly and imagine meeting with the client in a calm, relaxed manner, listening intently so I may understand his business needs and issues. This calm, attentive listening is the first step toward building a relationship and I can imagine having that meeting over and over again.

After preparing in my imagination, it comes time to meet the prospect. Whenever I've used this visualization technique, the meeting goes so much better. I'm more relaxed and in tune with the prospect because I've already had this meeting in my mind numerous times. My relaxed but attentive listening tends to create a more open and trusting atmosphere, which results in a better environment for relationship building.

Recall the talented athletes mentioned earlier. They practice and refine their skills daily. They also invest a substantial amount of time visualizing the big hit, the perfect swing, and ultimate success in crucial game and tournament situations. I call it the "visualize to actualize" way to practice your very best outcomes.

Visualization is a form of practice that will help you achieve success in whatever you do, whether it's speaking in front of people, improving your golf swing, or becoming more efficient at routine tasks. Visualization should become part of your ritual for continuous improvement.

Considered the greatest diver of all time, Greg Louganis won more than forty national and international titles. He is probably best known for sweeping the springboard and platform gold medals in both the 1984 and 1988 Olympic Games. He was favored to win both events in 1980, before the Moscow Olympics were boycotted by the United States. Many may not be aware that an integral component to Greg's success was his extensive use of visualization. Greg used the visualization tool as a way to learn the most difficult dives. In his memoir, Breaking the Surface, he says, "I would do every step over and over in my head until I visualized getting it right.... By practicing over and over again in my head I stopped worrying about going blank. I had the routine so deeply memorized that I could feel it."[6]

[6] Greg Louganis and Eric Marcus, Breaking the Surface (New York: Plume, 1996).

By visualizing our desired outcome over and over again, we become better prepared to achieve our desired outcome. Practice makes perfect, whether real or imagined. Whether we're a banker, teacher, or pro athlete, visualization is a type of simulation proven to expand our success. In fact, visualization is a form of perfect practice where we see ourselves utilizing our unique gifts at their highest levels.

Trust Yourself, Trust Others

Building up our strengths has a dual purpose. First and foremost, focusing on our strengths builds our self-confidence. In his book *Release Your Brakes*,[7] James Newman coins the term "comfort zone" and makes the key point that living outside our comfort zone is the only way we'll expand our comfort zone. For example, say you have identified a core strength as communication; however, your comfort zone in communicating is one-on-one or in very small groups. You would like to build on this strength, but in order to do so you will need to expand your comfort zone.

There are many ways you could do this both through visualization and practice. Through visualization you could see yourself speaking in front of large groups, feeling comfortable and connecting with the audience. For practice, you could join a local Toastmasters group or Rotary Club and hone your speaking skills in a supportive environment. Step-by-step, you're expanding your comfort zone and taking a small strength and building it into a formidable one. You will absolutely become more effective as a person by focusing on your strengths and working to enhance them through practice and visualization.

As you become a more effective and confident person, a second but equally important change begins to occur; the quiet confidence in your abilities allows you to be more accepting of others. Consider your

[7] James Newman, Release Your Brakes (Del Mar: Pace Organization, 1995).

work, where you encounter daily challenges dealing with customers, colleagues, subordinates, and managers. The world is made up of interdependent teams. Even most large organizations now have flat structures where people must work with colleagues from other areas in order to achieve internal and external objectives. Your job is probably dependent on you being effective dealing with others.

You know the old saying, "You can't love someone else until you love yourself." This may be trite, but it's absolutely true. You and I are not finished products, but we must have a baseline of belief, confidence, and security in ourselves before we'll be able to reach out and work effectively with others. The longer I live and work, the more I appreciate the differences in those with whom I work. We all have incredible gifts to offer, and learning to seek out those strengths in others takes a feeling of confidence and inner security that can only be achieved through a core belief in self.

Ongoing Control of the Judging Mind

By focusing on our strengths, we're controlling our conscious and Judging Mind. Instead of filling our minds with thoughts of insecurity, deficiency, and negativity, we practice and visualize success utilizing our unique gifts. This repetition is vital for successful living. According to Ralph Waldo Emerson, the great American poet, philosopher, and essayist of the nineteenth century, "A man [or woman] is what he [she] thinks about all day long."

"A man is what he thinks about all day long."
– Ralph Waldo Emerson

Ongoing control of our Judging Mind and its condemning self-talk is necessary in order to make lasting change in our behavior. However, the Judging Self has become such an inseparable part of how most of us see ourselves, we must be vigilant in maintaining control and recognize that our Natural Self is indeed separate from and usually obscured by the Judging Mind.

We live a dual existence. Our conscious or Judging Mind is the existence most of us are fully aware of, but equally important is the subconscious, spiritual, and infinite mind (I will use these terms interchangeably). Each of us has access to these levels of consciousness through the Natural Self; however, the Judging Mind is oblivious to their existence.

The Judging Mind is very handy for everyday problem solving at work or school. In fact, our schools and work training focus almost exclusively on our Judging Mind. But as we learned in the beginning of this section, our Judging Mind can be very negative and get in the way of learning who we really are unless we take charge of our self-discovery. Our Judging Mind works all the time; yet it's up to us to determine when it must shut down in order to make room for our Natural Self.

The self-condemning, negative talk we internalize through our Judging Mind is often based on limited material. For this reason we must discover our strengths, visualize our successes, and with effort develop our unique gifts. These methods work wonders in the deep recesses of our infinite and subconscious minds, which incorporate our experiences and reflects those experiences back to us in a kind of feedback mechanism.

Dr. Joseph Murphy's book *The Power of Your Subconscious Mind*[8] expresses how this feedback mechanism works.

What is your idea or feeling about yourself now? Every part of your being expresses that idea. Your vitality, body, financial condition, friends, and social status represent a perfect reflection of the idea you

[8] Joseph Murphy, The Power of Your Subconscious Mind (New York: Bantam, 2001), pg. 40.
9 Ibid, pg. 7.

have of yourself. This is the real meaning of what is impressed in your subconscious mind and what is expressed in all phases of your life.

It's vital, therefore, that we control our conscious, Judging Mind. Dr. Murphy goes on to say, "This is the reason it is so essential that you take charge of your thoughts. In that way, you can bring forth only desirable conditions."[9] We decide whether we want to incorporate negativity, lack, or bitterness. Our Judging Mind takes in whatever limited information it has experienced and it's internalized by the subconscious mind regardless of its truth. There is a saying, "garbage in, garbage out." We won't be able to reach the highest levels of performance without a focused and disciplined approach to what we choose to reflect on.

Discovery of unique gifts and strengths is the foundation for our internal sense of value and self-worth. By choosing to focus on our gifts and strengths, we begin the process of living a more fulfilling life. Then we can build up and refine these gifts through a variety of life-affirming tools and strategies.

Key Takeaways:
1. Focus on your strengths, but be aware of your weaknesses, which are often the flipside of our strengths.

2. Self 1 and Self 2 describe the dual existence of the Judging Self and the Natural Self inside every one of us.

3. The Judging Self is the primary mode in which we experience life. It tends to take on the characteristics of our worst teacher, coach, or critical parent.

4. The Natural Self is the doer and is quite sensitive to negative or critical self-talk. The Natural Self is closest to our "true self" and often becomes obscured by the wishes or desires of our parents, friends, or society.

5. Quieting the Judging Self is critical in allowing the Natural Self to discover its unique gifts and strengths.

6. We can hone our strengths through practice. We'll only expand the "comfort zone" by moving out of the comfort zone, essentially expanding beyond our prior abilities.

7. Utilize the Benjamin Franklin approach to self-improvement. Incorporate practice into your daily life by scheduling it on your calendar.

8. Visualize to actualize. By visualizing perfect success over and over again, our subconscious is able to experience that success as though it actually occurred.

9. The more confidence and trust we have in ourselves, the better able we are to deal effectively with people. This is a key driver to success in our life's work.

10. Negative self-talk is poisonous. Our goal is to quiet the Judging Mind while reaffirming our gifts in our subconscious mind.

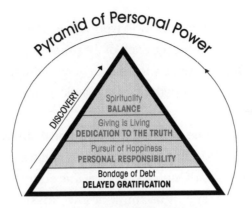

CHAPTER 2

DELAYED
GRATIFICATION

*"The ability to discipline yourself in the short term
in order to enjoy greater rewards in the long term
is the indispensable prerequisite for success."*
– Brian Tracy

The first chapter focused on the recognition (re: to bring; cognition: thinking or awareness) of our unique gifts and strengths. Once we uncover the talents of the Natural Self, we may next focus on the development of these qualities. The process of discovery takes us up the steps of the Pyramid of Personal Power, the first of which is delayed gratification.

Delayed gratification is nothing more than a habit—the habit of doing those things we least enjoy first, followed by those things we find more enjoyable or satisfying next. At first, we may find this habit difficult to master. Think back on any project you started that seemed extremely difficult: learning how to type, mastering a foreign language, or memorizing lines for a play. Each of these activities required *focused effort or discipline* in order to master. Over time, and through a disciplined approach of repetition and practice, the skill developed and became a habit.

What thoughts come to mind when you hear the word discipline? For many of us it's effort, punishment, labor, and training. Perhaps the word conjures images of military officers marching in perfect unison. Alternatively, how many of us think of love, mastery, and evolution when discipline is discussed? Discipline is at the heart of each of these words. Without discipline, we simply cannot have love, mastery, and evolution. At the core of each of these words is action and a willingness to extend oneself to be better. In addition, each of these words requires focus, intention, and attention. We only improve by developing a habit of awareness of how we live our lives.

If asked to choose between being spontaneous or being disciplined, many would select spontaneity. Even though our culture glorifies spontaneity, the habit of discipline allows a much more fruitful life. Of course, being disciplined does not preclude being spontaneous on occasion. Being disciplined is rarely extolled in our "get it now" society, but instead of seeing discipline as a rigid approach to life, we must recognize it as the ultimate act of love.

Discipline is the ultimate act of love.

American Heritage Dictionary defines self-discipline as: "Training and control of oneself and one's conduct, usually for personal improvement." Through the process of discovery we become more aware of who we are, including our strengths and weaknesses. By using the tools of discipline and delayed gratification, we prepare ourselves for a life of abundance. These tools are in sync with the laws of nature that surround us—perhaps best exemplified in the farming process.

The Farmer

Even those who have little or no experience in farming (including me) can identify the basic steps involved in successfully growing a crop: preparing, planting, growing, and harvesting. Each step breaks down into numerous sub-tasks. For example, in the preparation stage, the farmer buys the seed, fertilizer, and other tools needed to grow a specific plant. During this stage, the farmer evaluates which crop makes the most sense to grow based on the suitability of the land and needs of the market. Then the soil is plowed, and if appropriate, fertilizer is added to nourish the soil and to maximize crop yield.

During the planting phase, the farmer plants at the appropriate depth and distances based on his experience of growing that specific crop. As the plants grow, the farmer spends significant time and great care tending the crop (weeding, watering, etc.). The process continues throughout the growing season until the crop is ready for harvest, which is the reward for all the discipline and effort invested in nurturing seeds into healthy plants.

The farming process follows natural laws that must be obeyed in order to grow a successful crop. Jesus used multiple farming parables in his teachings precisely because farming is a metaphor for living, and just about everyone during Jesus' time was intimately aware of the natural laws that governed farming. Just as a farmer is free to choose whether or not to follow the natural laws required to grow and harvest a successful crop, each of us is free to choose whether or not to pursue the natural laws of delayed gratification. You see, in the long run, there is no such thing as instant gratification; it's only a mirage that brings long-term pain and frustration. Delayed gratification is the process each of us must use in our own lives to achieve those things most important to us.

When we use the tools of discipline and delayed gratification, we'll find a similar cycle in achieving those goals most important in our lives. The harvest is the reward for taking much time and care in tending the crop, but it comes at the end. Just as there are no shortcuts in farming, there are no shortcuts in using the tools of delayed gratification. Nature rewards us at the end for our efforts, not at the beginning or in the middle.

For many crops, the farming cycle is a few months. However, the cycle for achieving a goal using the tools of delayed gratification may take much longer. Depending on what you want to achieve in your life, the cycle may last years rather than months. We'll discuss ways to insert milestone goals and rewards to keep ourselves engaged and not susceptible to discouragement. The important thing to remember is that discipline and delayed gratification are natural laws. Very little may be achieved in life without mastering delayed gratification.

Deeper Understanding

Do you eat the icing or the cake first? Do you do the tasks at work you least enjoy prior to doing those things you enjoy most? Delaying gratification is at the foundation of discipline and successful living, yet many of us have deeply ingrained habits that make it difficult to practice.

How many times have you seen a dress or new pair of shoes you just "had to have?" Rather than waiting to make the purchase, you buy them now. You get a brief moment of euphoria, but the newness quickly wears off and it's on to the next thing. This same cycle is often repeated in many other areas of our lives.

My wife and I were struggling with the very issues of discipline and delayed gratification with our son, Jack. Jack is a wonderful eleven-year-old boy who loves baseball, Xbox, and more recently, music. He received an iPod for Christmas and a new game for his Xbox called Rock Band. Jack was convinced he wanted a real electric guitar and lessons to learn how to play. He has never shown any interest in music before, so my wife and I didn't want to discourage him. However, we were aware of how he and his younger sister hop from one "gotta have" toy to another. Their rooms are a testament to how quickly they tire of the most recent toy and want the next thing. We felt it was important for Jack to have a stake in the purchase of his new guitar, but didn't want the lesson to be solely about money.

It just so happened that Jack had started baseball season. This was a big season for him. He would be in the older age group in his Mustang League and he really wanted to move on to the Bronco level, while being among the best in the league. Despite this desire, I found him lacking the will to do some key things needed to prepare for the season. He was more interested playing Xbox and rarely wanted to play catch with me (also his coach) or do batting practice.

We had a nice set-up in the basement that allowed him to practice his bat speed using the Quick Swing tool. I asked him why he didn't hit the Quick Swing any more. He replied it was so boring being down in the basement by himself. I said, "Well you can hit fifty balls in about twenty minutes; that doesn't seem long." We had a standing deal that if he hit fifty balls a day, seven days a week, I would pay him $10 a week. That seemed to me to be a lot of money for doing something he presumably enjoyed. I said, "You could make a lot of money during baseball season just doing your Quick Swing every day." He replied, "Well Dad, I don't really care about money. I don't need it."

At that moment I realized he was exactly right. I had it all wrong. Nobody "needs" money. What we need (and many times just want) isn't money, but what we can buy with money. Jack got everything he needed (and many of those things he wanted) from Mom and Dad. That is precisely how it should be, but as our children get older, they begin having more wants and desires, and if we do not teach delayed gratification at a relatively early age, they will expect these things right away, with as little effort as possible.

After my "Ah-ha!" moment, I saw this as a great opportunity to teach Jack the principle of delayed gratification. I said, "Jack, I know you don't need money, but you want that new guitar and guitar lessons. If you commit to doing your Quick Swing every day, I will credit $20 toward the purchase of the guitar each week (the one he wanted cost $160). I will split the cost of the guitar with you, so in four weeks, you'll have enough money to get the guitar. We'll look into the cost for the guitar lessons, and I will split that cost with you as well."

He was happy. I had given him a specific goal with defined rules to achieve it successfully. I was happy, because I had a son who was motivated to do his Quick Swing and follow through with the guitar lessons. He now had some "skin in the game," and it really motivated him in both areas of his life. When the four weeks were up, he was rewarded with a new guitar and he started the season as our hottest hitter. Achieving both goals was a good lesson for him.

Goal Setting and Achieving

Jack isn't the only one who struggles with setting and achieving goals. We all do! A common example most of us can relate to is New Year's resolutions. I'm an avid fitness fan and always dread the first few weeks after the New Year. The gym is always full of people attempting to fulfill perhaps the most popular resolution of all—losing weight and getting fit. I find that by about mid-February the gym gets back to the normal crowd. Why is this? Because many who made the resolution found it was difficult to maintain and came up with excuses why they could not follow through on their resolutions.

Although fitness wasn't on my list, I had trouble keeping my own resolutions. Each time the New Year rolled around, I had ambitious plans for what I was going to accomplish in the coming year. Here are some examples of New Year's resolutions that never quite got off the ground:

1. Develop an auto review website that provided news and reviews on all cars
2. Get a used auto dealer's license so I could buy and sell exotic cars
3. Win the sales award for my division at work
4. Read the entire Bible
5. Pray and meditate daily

These are just the more notable misses on my New Year's list, but the actual list goes on and on. As I reflect on it now, I had three problems with my goal setting: specificity, accountability, and milestone rewards. These goals did not lack ambition. If anything, they were so ambitious that achieving them was extremely difficult.

The biggest obstacle to achieving goals is their size; yet, we do not want to be limited to smaller, less-ambitious goals. The key is to develop sub-goals and milestone rewards to make larger goals more achievable. It's human nature to stare up at a large goal or obstacle and view it as a wholly insurmountable challenge. Breaking it down into something more bite-sized makes all the difference. This in effect narrows the gap between the goal and its achievement.

Here is how I approach my goal setting now. First, I spend some time between Christmas and New Year's Day to set my goals. I find this is a personal time of reflection and a week when I have days off from work, so it makes sense to invest time in goal setting. I reflect on those big areas in my life: God and spirituality, family, career, and personal development. Then I take a page out of David Letterman's Late Show and come up with my personal "Top Ten list."

I've included my goals for 2010 below. I make an effort to be specific and achievable—nothing pie-in-the-sky. In fact, the two are related; the more specific you are in formulating goals, the more likely you will be to incorporate them into everyday life planning and actually achieving the goals.

My 2010 goals did not overreach; they were not expansive. Instead, these goals represented first, second, or third steps in achieving bigger goals. For example, I did not have "writing a book" as one of my goals for 2010. It was simply too big and I had no idea how long it would take. I did not want to set myself up for failure. So, instead, I created two very specific sub-goals around my ultimate goal of writing a book: 1) develop a detailed book outline; 2) set aside two hours each week to write. Both goals were specific, measurable, and within my power to achieve. These goals became the foundation on which I built toward my overarching goal of writing a book.

2010 Goals
1. Read the New Testament
2. Read six success books
3. Develop a detailed book outline
4. Plan each week on Sunday
5. Be positive and expect the best
6. Invest time with Kim (cooking, date night ideas, etc.)
7. One special family day each month (camping, museums, etc.)
8. Do a special trip with Dani
9. Eliminate bitterness from my thinking
10. Set aside two hours each week to write

These are very personal goals, and you may find some of them strange or even a bit silly. I'm trying to create positive habits as much as anything. When you consider the amazing adventure that is life, remember you do not have to solve all of your problems today. Taking incremental steps toward those things that are most important to you will give you great satisfaction. For example, it's not enough for me to read the New Testament. Instead, I really want to search for the deep meanings and wisdom contained in Scripture. However, I have to start somewhere, and reading the New Testament is a start. Perhaps next year I will include a goal to read more about the history of the New Testament or its interpretation.

Framed for Success

At the heart of successfully setting and achieving goals is this maxim, "If it's going to be, it's up to me." For this reason, I take the additional step of putting my goals on paper and framing them in a picture frame. I set the frame next to my sink in the bathroom. There is no escaping my goals. Every morning and evening when I brush my teeth, shave, or wash my face, I have my goals staring at me. They might remind me that we have not done a family day in six weeks—I need to fix that! Or that I haven't had a date night with Kim in three weeks.

If it's going to be, it's up to me.

If you're not running your life, your life will run you. I know of no better way to stay on top of the most important things than by being accountable to our goals. If framed goals don't make sense for you, try something different. I'm aware of people that create "dream boards." These boards may take different forms, but the idea is to develop a picture of each of your core goals or dreams and post them someplace where you're reminded of them frequently. For example, if you have a goal to get fit, post a picture of someone in good shape exercising. If your goal is to save a certain amount of money for a down payment on a car or house, illustrate the saving idea with a bank logo and the picture of your dream house.

The advantage of the dream board is that it allows us to visualize our goals as well as the positive feelings associated with achieving them. As we discussed in the first chapter, visual images make an indelible impression on the subconscious mind and Natural Self. But setting goals and creating dream boards will not be enough; we must incorporate our goals into everyday life. Otherwise, we'll find ourselves looking at last year's goals on New Year's Day and feeling regret for what we could have done but didn't.

Time Management

Good time-management skills are a key determinant of whether or not we achieve our goals. In fact, my goal setting is a form of time management; I call it macro-time management. Each goal is designed to be accomplished in a year. Next, I focus on micro-time management; what I need to accomplish each week to enable me to be effective in my life's activities, as well as to accomplish my top goals. Here's what I do to achieve my micro-goals.

1. Plan each week on Sunday: Every Sunday evening, I spend twenty minutes planning for the week ahead and incorporating these plans into my task list for the week. First, I look at the prior week's task list and pick up any tasks that may not have been accomplished and put them into the coming week. Next, since I'm in business development, I set a goal of new clients I plan to call. Finally, I refer to my top ten goals and think about which one I want to focus on this week, and incorporate it into my schedule.

2. Incorporate at least one "big" goal into the week: The only way we'll accomplish our big resolutions is to incorporate them into our task list throughout the year. Some of my goals get incorporated into my daily life. For example, reading the New Testament would take considerable time, so I decided to read three chapters at the beginning of every working day whenever I wasn't traveling. My goals often require multiple steps to accomplish; therefore, I break them down into smaller steps and incorporate them into my weekly task list.

3. Do least favorite tasks first whenever possible: My least favorite task is cold-calling companies. It's a necessary evil to turn up leads, meet new prospects, and feed into business development. If I don't do it at the very beginning of my day, I don't do it at all. Cold-calling requires discipline. The only way I can cold-call is to do it at the start of the day, and I'm so glad when it's over! I can move on to the more enjoyable areas of my job. What's your least favorite task at work or at home? Develop a habit of completing that task first.

4. Stop watching TV and surfing the net: Jonathan Clements is one of my favorite *Wall Street Journal* contributors. He wrote about a new study that suggests Americans are no happier today than in prior generations despite an increased standard of living due to a poor use of leisure time. According to the study, we're most happy when we're fully engaged in conversation or activities with friends and family. In addition, we're happy when engaged in projects such as reading, working out, or fishing. Over the last forty years, we're doing far less of these things. The replacement? Television. How about working on your car or making jewelry (hobbies my wife and I enjoy) instead? Find projects or hobbies that fully engage you and stop watching TV. [10]

Rewarding Yourself at Harvest Time

Goal setting and time management skills are the core tools we should use in daily life to delay gratification. These tools are the "blocking and tackling" of successful execution. If we set good goals, incorporate them into weekly planning, and hold ourselves accountable to achieving them, we'll begin to see incredible changes

---

[10] Jonathan Clements, "Down the Tube: The Sad Stats on Happiness, Money, and TV," *Wall Street Journal*, April 2, 2008.

in our ability to execute. But where is the reward? Over the long term, say the next few years, we'll see enormous rewards in the form of more success at work, better relationships at home, and growing confidence in our skills and abilities. Success will result from the consistent setting and achieving of goals.

In much the same way I came up with the reward for Jack to give him some "skin in the game" for his guitar, you need to do the same for your goal setting and achieving. If each of your goals is important and worthy of focused effort, then achieving it should merit a reward. Once you complete a goal, reward yourself with a little something you want. Here are some examples of my goals and rewards:

2010 Goals	Rewards
Read the New Testament	Running shoes
Read six success books	Sports watch
Develop a detailed book outline	Sunglasses
Plan each week on Sunday	----
Be positive and expect the best	----
Invest time with Kim	----
One special family day each month	Bike pump
Do a special trip with Dani	Two new ties
Eliminate bitterness from my thinking	----
Set aside two hours each week to write	New book

Since the next level of our pyramid cannot be built until we achieve some consistency in delayed gratification, it's important that we build these habits into our daily lives. Delayed gratification challenges each of us to do better and to strive for more by extending ourselves beyond our comfort zones. I find I'm more fully engaged in life when I have a list of goals and dreams I'm actively pursuing. It's through pursuit of dreams that our lives become more exciting and fulfilling. This allows for meaningful growth through discovery of those things most important to us. Delayed gratification begins the process of growth by building a reward system for setting and achieving goals.

Intelligence and Delayed Gratification

According to an article in WebMD News, delayed gratification and intelligence are linked.[11] Researchers at Yale did a study on the connection between delayed gratification and intelligence and concluded that it had to do with the maturity of the anterior prefrontal cortex. The article quotes Noah A. Shamosh, PhD: "It has been known for some time that intelligence and self-control are related, but we didn't know why. Our study indicates the function of a specific brain structure, the anterior prefrontal cortex, which is one of the last areas of the brain to fully mature."

In the study, researchers presented 103 healthy adults a variety of scenarios having to do with financial rewards—trading a larger financial reward down the road for a smaller one today. Multiple dollar amounts and timing scenarios were tested. The participants then underwent a variety of intelligence and short-term memory tests followed by a day of similar tests while their brains were being scanned using a functional MRI. The people who scored the highest on the intelligence test and demonstrated the most restraint in the delayed gratification test also had the most activity show up on the MRI. "Understanding the factors that support better self-control is relevant to a host of important behaviors, ranging

[11] Caroline Wilbert, WebMD Health News, "Delayed Gratification, Intelligence Linked: Intelligence and Self Control Come From the Same Region of the Brain, New Research Shows." September 18, 2008.

from saving for retirement to maintaining physical and mental health," the authors conclude.

Anyone reading this book is intelligent enough to understand the importance of delayed gratification. Understanding the concept, however, isn't enough. We have to incorporate goal setting, time management, and milestone rewards into our daily lives. This is part of the awareness process discussed at the beginning of the book.

Once we take ownership of our life plans through goal setting and achieving, it becomes easier to say no to instant gratification. Shortcuts become less appealing because they take us off track. In short, we're taking more responsibility for our life's direction.

Key Takeaways:

1. Delayed gratification is the foundation of the Pyramid of Personal Power. It's central to successful living.

2. Self-discipline is the ultimate act of love.

3. Nature reveals the importance of delayed gratification through the farming cycle. The harvest comes at the end of a multi-step process without shortcuts.

4. Successful goal setting and achieving consciously use the principle of delayed gratification.

5. Set annual goals (macro-time management) and put them in a frame where you can refer to them frequently, or post them on a dream board.

6. At the heart of goal setting and achieving is the maxim, "If it's going to be, it's up to me."

7. Micro-time management is handled weekly and incorporates one of your annual goals into your week.

8. Do your least favorite task first, and limit your time with TV and the Internet.

9. Incorporate milestone rewards into your goal setting to keep focused throughout the year.

10. Delayed gratification is a muscle that must be exercised to gain strength to take control of our lives.

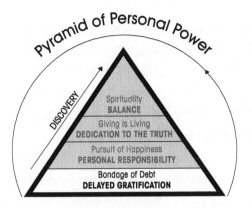

CHAPTER 3

BONDAGE OF DEBT

"A man in debt is so far a slave."
– Ralph Waldo Emerson

Although debt may not be as evil as Emerson suggests, its use in our society is a good measure of our collective ability to delay gratification. As we learned in the last chapter, delayed gratification is at the foundation of our Pyramid of Personal Power; therefore, it touches most aspects of our lives. At its core, delayed gratification allows us to improve and evolve by dispensing rewards based on achievement of set goals. We delay gratification when we do our least favorite tasks first. We delay gratification when we save to buy the ring, rather than putting it on the credit card and carrying a balance. Delayed gratification uses the timeless principles of pleasure and pain to attain what's important in our lives.

How would you grade yourself in a test of delayed gratification? One of the best ways to measure individual as well as society's collective ability to carry out this foundational discipline is to take a look at the amount of debt we carry as a nation. When we examine household debt and gross domestic product (GDP) over the last ninety years, we see household debt between 50 and 70 percent of GDP during most of that time. There were only two years in which household debt is 100 percent of GDP: those years are 1929 and 2007, both of which preceded unprecedented economic declines.

Although most economists agree that we will likely not encounter a depression as severe as the 1930s, the Great Recession of 2008 is likely to have a long-term, negative impact on individual households and our economy as a whole. According to David Beim, professor at Columbia University, "We have been living very high on the hog. Our living standard has been rising dramatically in the last 25 years. And we have been borrowing much of the money to make that prosperity happen." [12]

We're a nation and a people in debt and the incredible amount of debt we carry impacts our ability to live consistently with our guiding principles. The more we buy, the more we want until we discover that we have put ourselves into a hole so deep we limit our ability to live a fulfilling life. We find ourselves trapped in a job and a lifestyle where we may have many material objects we desire except for the one thing we truly need: an ability to pursue our guiding principles resulting in true peace and fulfillment.

The House

I'll never forget that rainy day sitting in a Chili's restaurant after church and calling a Realtor about a house I had seen online. This had become routine for Kim and me in late 2005 (not church, but house-hunting), and eating out was the bribe that kept our kids somewhat cooperative. The house was $100,000 more than the houses we were looking at in nearby neighborhoods and more than twice what I

---

[12] Laura Conaway, "Household Debt vs. GDP," National Public Radio Planet Money Blog, February 27, 2009.

expected to sell our house for. I couldn't believe I was actually going to look at such an expensive house. In fact, Kim did not want to look at it because she was convinced she would fall in love with a house we could not afford. Her instincts were right.

Home values at that time were near their peak; interest rates were low, and creative financing was all the rage. Since we fully expected to get near our asking price for our existing house, I had calculated the maximum I thought we could afford. Clearly, this house was on the edge of the affordability range, but I was a banker, and I knew the angles to play in the mortgage market. For example, I knew we would have to do a five-year interest-only mortgage to afford the house. Since it had been on the market for a while, I negotiated a contract with a contingency that my house had to sell prior to close. Unfortunately, as most contingencies go, this one had a kick-out clause if anyone else put a contract on the house.

You can see where this is going. I did too, in kind of a slow-motion, surreal way. After signing the contract in January of 2006, we put our house on the market. No more than a week after that, we had a decision to make. Another contract was placed on the house that we had fallen head over heels for, the kick-out was triggered, and we had to decide whether to remove the contingency. Because the house was not yet finished, our closing date was May 5, which felt a world away from dreary January. Besides, the house we were selling was beautiful and Kim had a flair for decorating that made the place stand out.

When I look back on the situation now, we had chances to back out of the pickle we placed ourselves in. As the closing on the new house rapidly approached without our current house selling, we had some decisions to make.

As I write this book, the housing and credit bubbles have burst and we now realize that the appreciation we saw in real estate over the last ten years was a mirage. My guess is that our story played out across the country with numerous buyers and sellers buying bigger and thinking it would be better. In light of this, we should remember Immutable Law 3:

IMMUTABLE LAW 3
No manner of material possessions will ever satisfy the longing and craving in our hearts.

Kim and I finally sold our house on September 29, 2006. I remember that date well because it also happens to be my son's birth date—what a great birthday present! The home building and selling process had lasted for the better part of a year, and we carried both houses for five months. Those were the longest five months of our lives, and it took us two years to fully recover financially from the purchase of our dream house.

Do we love our house? Yes. Was it worth it? From a financial perspective, I don't know yet, but most likely, no. Would I do it again? No way! Here's why. Even though we were able to stretch to make it work, the financial strain the new house placed (and will continue to place) on us is a high price for Kim and me to pay.

Ultimately, we have much more house than we'll ever need. Where does it end? We're now used to our big house and have moved on to new goals such as furnishing the house, getting new cars, etc. The more I accumulate in material wealth, the more I realize the continuous cycle of material desire only ends when I take a disciplined stand on spending.

Dark Side of Blessing

We're blessed to live in a time where so much is possible.

Advancements in technology are changing the way goods and services are delivered the world over. The underpinnings of the U.S. economy, capitalism and property rights, are the best model for creating wealth and abundance in society. As a result, we're surrounded by a vast array of goods and services designed to "improve" our lives.

The dark side of our consumer culture is the constant barrage of advertisements appealing to our ego desires and insecurities. We simply can't live without the latest car, television, or designer clothes. We are a society locked in battle with our neighbors for the next great material goal, but it's vital we remain cognizant of another immutable law regarding the wealth "arms race." Whenever we strive for material wealth alone, we will never be satisfied. "Stuff" can never fill the hole inside.

IMMUTABLE LAW 4
Whenever we strive for material wealth alone, we will never be satisfied.

So why do we do it? Why do we move from one material desire to the next? It's common in our society to use material wealth as a yardstick to measure the success of people. Presumably, the wealthier people are, the more intelligent, resourceful, and successful they are.

Or are they?

Whenever we start with the desire for the next material goal, we experience a brief satisfaction in its achievement, but the satisfaction is nearly always fleeting and we move on quickly to the next material desire. Seldom do we ask if the job we have or the goals we pursue are in sync with our guiding principles. Work becomes a means to a material end, and when we work from one material want to the next, we begin to lose our true selves.

In much the same way Emerson said, we become slaves to our ego or mind desires without taking a step back and considering what's most important to us. The ego becomes addicted to the feeling of material achievement, no matter how fleeting. Don't get me wrong. I recognize the value of goals—see the previous chapter. Material goals are valuable motivators. However, for true peace and happiness, they cannot be our sole motivators. We'll never be able to achieve inner peace while we're only satisfying our outer material desires.

If we can understand and become totally conscious of the cycle of human behavior that drives these decisions, we can regain control. Why wait for a mid-life crisis to become conscious of our habits? Although the subject of jokes, a mid-life crisis is sparked by the belief that we are trapped or lack control in our lives. Many fight back by making surprising decisions about new-car purchases or worse, divorce. Why allow our egos to drive our decision making in an unconscious way?

My fascination with this subject began more than five years ago when I asked my dad, "Is this all there is?" He was a bit shocked by my question, given my outward appearance of material success. But as I've found, material success often results in feelings of dissatisfaction and disconnection. Our mind tells us that when we attain the next promotion or the next bonus, we can get the _____ (boat, car, ring, watch) we've wanted our whole life. Don't fall for the mirage at the expense of peace, satisfaction, and joy.

Temporary Satisfaction of Ego

My own demons in dealing with material wants start and stop with cars. As early as I can remember, I've loved cars. I collected and played with Matchbox and Hot Wheels cars as a young boy, built car models as an adolescent, and began driving my own car as soon as I got my license at sixteen. Although my ownership of cars had a humble beginning (my first car was a 1981 Ford Escort), I've owned more cars as a forty-year-old than most people will own in a lifetime—nineteen to be exact. That's insane! As I've gotten older and been able to afford the cars I always dreamed of owning as a child, the models have become more exotic: BMW 550i, BMW M5, and Porsche C4S.

Each time I bought a car, I experienced a great deal of satisfaction. I would spend countless Sundays washing and waxing my new prized possession and had great fun driving on the back roads of Georgia, putting it through its paces. I genuinely enjoyed and appreciated the car; however, there was always a time about six months later when the newness wore off. I would go back to reading my car magazines and trolling the Internet for my next prize. The amount of money I've thrown at this expensive hobby is ridiculous. It's one thing if you have vast resources to indulge in this hobby, but quite another when you don't. I certainly didn't have the resources to indulge my hobby to the extent I did.

We're a "buy today, pay tomorrow" culture that has never been so stretched by our desire to consume, to upgrade, and to keep up with the Joneses. Think about the constant barrage of solicitations we receive by direct mail, by e-mail, and from the credit card companies. As a result, we're charging ourselves into oblivion through an insatiable desire for that next new thing.

To change our habits, we need to understand the psychology behind our behavior and then develop new habits that effectively harness our minds to work in concert with our guiding principles rather than our ego-driven material wants. You know from the previous chapters that I'm a big believer in creating new positive habits. It's much easier to create new habits than it is to stop old habits. So, we'll look to create new habits designed to harness the psychology behind our behavior—what I call the "Treadmill Effect."

The Treadmill Effect

The Treadmill Effect is a feedback mechanism in which we expend effort or experience pain in order to achieve a pleasurable outcome. This feedback loop, used by our ego or mind, has a huge impact on the personal and professional goals we set. However, these goals are often set unconsciously based on the values or beliefs of our parents, friends, or society as a whole. Instead of allowing the desires of the ego to go unchecked or to be set unconsciously, we must consciously create a new set of goals and discipline our minds to build habits in sync with these goals. We can use the principles of the Treadmill Effect to control our use of debt and allow us to attain financial freedom. Finally, we'll explore how to leverage financial freedom into personal freedom as we begin to live in accordance with our guiding principles.

Delayed gratification and self-discipline are achieved through consciousness and control. By consciousness, I mean understanding what motivates us and why. By control, I mean taking ownership of developing and pursuing goals that are in sync with our guiding principles. Many of us live by the mantra, "If it feels good, do it." Then we wonder why we make the same mistakes over and over again with colleagues, friends, and family. We blame others for our misfortunes and believe that very little is within our control. Life becomes a vicious circle of frustration, which may turn into resentment and bitterness over time.

The Treadmill Effect is the natural way our minds set and achieve goals. Rather than fighting our natural goal-setting mechanism, the purpose of this chapter is to make us aware of how our minds and bodies work and then use this awareness to gain more control over our lives, specifically in regard to the way we spend money.

Humans are on a constant quest to seek pleasure and avoid pain. Although we would like to do only pleasurable activities, over the years we have learned that some effort or pain is required to attain the pleasure we seek. If I want to enjoy tennis or golf, I have to put in time practicing in order to get better and enjoy the sport.

Most of us realize that in order to have a house, a car, or obtain an education, we must work at a job, and for most of us, that job involves considerable effort and in many cases, pain. The Treadmill Effect is a reward mechanism that the mind uses in seeking pleasure. It is willing to sacrifice time and effort for the ultimate payoff. I call it the Treadmill Effect because it works similarly to going to the gym and running on the treadmill. The Treadmill Effect also speaks to doing the same thing over and over and not getting anywhere—more on that later.

As part of my workout routine, I usually spend thirty minutes on the treadmill. I run for a little over three miles, so I'm not setting any pace records. In fact, I don't like running at all. I would rather do nearly anything other than running on the treadmill, but I do it because I think it's good for me physically and because I'm addicted to the feeling after the workout. The natural high I achieve after running is a direct result of the release of endorphins, the body's natural pain-killers.

As it is with the treadmill at the gym, so it is on the treadmill of life. The mind sets a pleasure goal, achieves that goal, and achieves a temporary high from it. But just like the endorphins released by a physical workout, the sense of satisfaction is fleeting. The mind forces us to move on to the next ego-satisfying goal. The same natural high experienced after exercise is also achieved after the satisfaction of other ego or mind desires. The primary difference is that we often pursue these desires unconsciously. The first step in delayed gratification is to use the Treadmill Effect consciously just as we do when we work out, eat sensibly, or complete that difficult task at work.

Conscious and Unconscious

The good news about the Treadmill Effect is that the mind and body are willing to sacrifice something in order to attain the pleasure it wants (delayed gratification). The trouble comes when: a) we're not conscious of the choices we're making with this feedback and reward system; or b) we skip the effort-filled piece and only seek the pleasurable activity.

Setting and achieving goals was an area of strength for me and my discipline allowed me to achieve some material goals that I would not have achieved otherwise. Upon reflection of many of the big purchases I made, however, I realized I was not conscious as to the motivators associated with these purchases. I was not thinking about how these purchases would limit me and the family in other aspects of our lives.

Think about your own pleasure-seeking activities. Are they causing pleasure or pain in your life? What are your mind's addictions? Is it the rush that comes from going out to a club on Friday night after a long week at work? Is it going shopping on a Saturday to relieve the stress brought on by the work week? Are you attracted to the same type of person over and over again despite that personality type creating all sorts of friction and pain? Albert Einstein once said, "The definition of insanity is doing the same thing over and over again and expecting different results."

When you take a step back and evaluate your decisions, you will find that, without exception, you make decisions based on this pleasure/pain principle. This is powerful knowledge and the first step in utilizing this mind behavior pattern consciously rather than subconsciously. When we use the principle of the Treadmill Effect consciously, we have the ability to move our decisions away from the ongoing accumulation of material goods and into more rewarding goal setting that is congruent with our guiding principles.

Now let's focus on some practical challenges that the pleasure/pain principle brings through the accumulation of material possessions.

The Pull of Materialism

The pull of materialism is strong. Most people would agree that living in a big, spacious house with large bedrooms and multiple bathrooms would be far more comfortable that living in a cramped mobile home. Or, that driving a Porsche is far more enjoyable that driving a Ford Escort. However, once we achieve the key components of shelter, transportation, and a stable, fulfilling job, should a family making $100,000 per year be more or less fulfilled than the family making $1,000,000? We have all seen it, and most of us experience it. No matter how much money we make, for many of us, there is always a desire for more. Why?

We all have a *need to feel important.*

Materialism is the fast food of personal fulfillment. The car, the clothes, and the house are outward, visible signs of our success, even though they do not nourish or fulfill our guiding principles. Our consumer culture celebrates these outward signs of success, but materialism is a poor substitute for true personal growth and fulfillment. We may be able to temporarily meet the needs of self-esteem or importance by buying newer, fancier things, but ultimately there is a price to pay. Just as fast food can have long-term implications for our physical health, consumerism has long-term implications for our mental well-being. What most of us do not realize is that materialism is used as a crutch to our self-esteem from early childhood and is ever-present in our decision-making today.

Lan Nguyen Chaplin (University of Illinois) and Deborah Roedder John (University of Minnesota) did a study featured in the Journal of Consumer Research that shows that low self-esteem and materialism are not only correlated but causally related in children. In other words, low self-esteem causes materialism and raising self-esteem decreases materialism. Their study grouped kids by age group (8-9, 12-13, and 16-18) and asked them to make collages on paper plates about what made them happy. Some children were given paper plates on which their peers had written positive comments or attributes about them. The children who made the collages after reading their positive attributes were much less materialistic than those who did not. The materialistic wants of these children were a crutch to their self-esteem.[13]

Adolescence is probably the most challenging time for maintaining our self-esteem. It's when many of our habits, patterns, and values are formed—often subconsciously. These values are then carried into adulthood with little awareness, yet they drive our decisions in many ways.

Delayed gratification is an important tool in regaining that self-esteem. Tools of delayed gratification such as family budgets, goal setting/achievement, and task-list accomplishment place us in control of our actions. When we become conscious and take back control, our self-esteem improves immeasurably. The cycle of materialism—desire, buy, repeat—is very similar to a drug or alcohol addiction. Breaking that addiction gives us a renewed sense of accomplishment.

Commit to a Family Budget

There are many fine books that provide step-by-step instruction for developing, measuring, and sticking with a family budget. These specifics are outside the scope of this book. However, each of the books I've read on the topic use the tools of discipline and delayed gratification—and, in many cases, the Treadmill Effect—to get an individual or family to live within their means. They use the principles of consciousness, control, and accountability as the cornerstones for making changes and living within budget constraints.

Since we're all different, there are multiple approaches that may be equally successful in managing money and budgets. What works for me may not work for you. However, I will share three key components

---

[13]Lan Nguyen Chaplin and Deborah Roedder John, Journal of Consumer Research, Inc., "Growing up in a Material World: Age Differences in Materialism in Children and Adolescents", December, 2007.

to my family's approach in hopes they will help you set and achieve success in your own budgeting process.

1. Accountability: Instead of a family budget, Kim and I each manage individual budgets. We have tried various family budgets many times, but they resulted in failure. Because it was a family budget, we had difficulty with individual accountability within that framework. It was only after we pushed responsibility to who had control of the various monthly costs that we began to stick to a family budget. Before handling our expenses in this way, we found payment of the monthly bills a very stressful event in which we would quiz each other on the various expenses we had the prior month. Once we set up individual budgets and split the responsibility, we found much of this stress disappeared.

2. Funny Money: In order to handle unexpected or discretionary purchases we set aside "funny money" for each of us. At the beginning of each year, we agree on the amount of funny money. We pay ourselves a set amount quarterly and use it for unexpected expenses or discretionary spending each of us may want to do without disrupting the family budget.

3. Rewards: This is a game I play with myself and my kids utilizing the Treadmill Effect. I set goals each year and attach small rewards to achieving them. The rewards aren't big and often they are things I may need such as new running shoes or clothes. However, the achievement of the goal and the subsequent reward reinforces a goal setting and achievement behavior. A child who has weekly chores that must be completed to receive an allowance is using the same principle. My son, Jack, really wanted an iPod Touch and his desire resulted in a new zeal for doing his chores. When he had finally saved up enough for the iPod, he found buying it much more rewarding.

Financial Freedom and Personal Freedom

Now back to the quote at the beginning of the chapter: "A man in debt is so far a slave." I chose that quote to make a point, but I do not subscribe unequivocally to it. As a banker, I see how the prudent use of debt allows companies to grow, hire more workers, and improve society as a whole. In fact, developing countries without an effective banking system are not able to grow and develop. Many countries have lost decades of growth and development by not being able to use credit to grow businesses and hire workers.

Perhaps no place in the world was more impacted by this negative vicious cycle than Bangladesh. Bangladesh's poverty is a complex, multi-faceted issue, but much can be traced back to three issues: lack of education, lack of services for the rural population, and gender inequalities. Perhaps no one understands better the situation than Dr. Muhammad Yunus who was born into extreme poverty in the small village of Bathua outside Chittagong, Bangladesh. Dr. Yunus was a bright young man and one of the lucky few who was able to study in the best schools in Chittagong. He went on to receive a Fulbright scholarship to study economics at Vanderbilt University and graduated in 1971.

Although his life in the United States was much easier, he never allowed himself to be removed from his roots, and after the Liberation War of Bangladesh was over, he returned home and became involved with poverty-reduction projects. Dr. Yunus found that very small loans could make a disproportionate difference to a poor person. His first loan—twenty-seven dollars from his own pocket—was made to forty-two women, and so began the process of unlocking value in small poor villages.

Dr. Yunus founded Grameen Bank, "Bank of the Villages," in 1976 to combat extreme poverty. In so doing, he created the concept of micro-credit to help these poor villages help themselves. The idea behind the bank was to make credit available to individuals within the village and rely on peer pressure and discipline of the local village to ensure repayment. The program has been incredibly successful in eradicating extreme poverty and supporting entrepreneurial business ventures. By 2006, Grameen Bank had grown to more than 2,100 branches. Its success has inspired similar projects in more than forty countries and has resulted in fundamental strategy changes at the World Bank.

Also in 2006, Grameen Bank and Dr. Yunus received the Nobel Peace Prize for their groundbreaking work. I bet you never thought a banker would win a Nobel Peace Prize!

I can't think of a better way to highlight the virtues of credit than through this story; however, even this virtuous credit cycle can break down. Just as too much of a good thing can be a bad thing, our own appetite for credit can become distorted. Rather than using credit to start and build a business, we began to use it to put money in our pockets. Instead of a means to an end, credit becomes the end in itself. Our houses and businesses became piggy banks to feed our insatiable appetite for material wants.

We forget the fundamentals behind credit and take on more credit to buy more things we ultimately don't need. We lose sight of our guiding principles and instead pursue gluttonous material desires. As individuals and as a country, we're paying the price for unchecked spending and use of credit.

Clearly, access to capital and the prudent use of credit have allowed our society to grow and become prosperous. However, the recent housing and credit bubble underscore how fragile our relationship with credit can be. Anything taken to excess or abused will negatively impact our future. It's in this context that Emerson's quote resonates most clearly for me. When our desire for more, better stuff eclipses our means, we begin to lose our personal freedom.

Vital Link

Financial freedom and personal freedom are inexorably linked. The less financial freedom we have, the less personal freedom we experience in our daily lives. When we feel as though we're not free, life becomes a stressful drudgery. Delayed gratification and the Treadmill Effect are methods by which we can consciously control what for many is an unconscious desire for things that can adversely impact our ability to attain financial freedom.

Whatever you do, don't confuse financial freedom with the lifestyles of the rich and famous, or tell yourself that you will change once you have the means to save more or pay down more debt. I've read compelling stories about school teachers, truck drivers, and janitors who are living a life with financial freedom. Conversely, I know many doctors, lawyers, and bankers who are in the bondage of debt.

The way you choose to live your life today—whether you have an abundance of money or very little—will quite likely stay with you for the rest of your life. Make financial freedom a goal today and live consistently with that goal. As you grow and develop in your chosen job or vocation, you will find that the ups and downs of your work life will become less stressful because you have chosen not to live from paycheck to paycheck or to be over-leveraged. Instead, a life of financial freedom will bring you much closer to personal freedom and a willingness to experiment with work and life. Our jobs become sources of fulfillment rather than prison sentences we must serve for the sins of materialism and debt.

Key Takeaways:

1. Society's collective ability to be able to delay gratification may be best measured by the amount of debt it carries. Only two times in our nation's history have we carried more debt than GDP: 1929 and 2007.

2. No amount of material possessions will ever satisfy the longing in our hearts. Only after discovering our unique purpose and guiding principles will we find peace and true satisfaction.

3. Our minds develop desires or cravings and we often go about satisfying them without considering the implications.

4. Once the mind achieves a material goal, the body experiences a brief moment of satisfaction before it moves on to the next desire.

5. The Treadmill Effect illustrates the mind and body's pain and pleasure principles that may be used consciously to achieve goals.

6. Delayed gratification and self-discipline are achieved through consciousness and control.

7. The pull of materialism is strong and at its core is a need to feel important. Society sees outward signs of material wealth as visible symbols of personal success. These symbols are often a veneer to make someone feel important.

8. Delayed gratification and the Treadmill Effect are essential for making a family budget work, as are the practical tools of accountability, funny money, and rewards.

9. Credit and debt are not evil in and of themselves, but their overuse has caused devastation to millions of people in the U.S.

10. Pursuing a path of financial freedom will result in a greater sense of personal freedom; the two are linked.

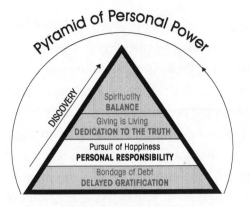

CHAPTER 4

ASSUMPTION OF RESPONSIBILITY

"Action springs not from thought,
but from a readiness for responsibility."
— Dietrich Bonhoeffer

The next level in the discipline pyramid is assumption of responsibility. How many times do we lament our bad luck or express envy at a friend or neighbor who has it made? Assuming responsibility for where we are at a given life stage can be difficult, because we all encounter setbacks and challenges. It's often easier to blame circumstances for failure, but until we accept total responsibility for our place in life, we'll never muster the will or discipline to make our position better.

Think about it; when we blame people or conditions for where we are now, we make ourselves dependent on people or conditions to be successful. Our dependence limits us, gives us an out, and saps our will from making the changes necessary to take us to the next level in life. Assuming personal responsibility is a breakthrough for people wanting the best out of themselves and the most out of life. They say, "I will encounter difficult decisions along the way, but I move forward in faith with a sense of purpose and responsibility."

In his book *The Road Less Traveled*, Scott Peck compares two personality types: the neurotic and the character disorder. In the simplest definitions, the neurotic takes on too much responsibility for negative life events and is constantly trying to change or become better at what he or she is doing. Although self-improvement is a worthy pursuit, and a key element of this book, the neurotic takes on an unhealthy amount of responsibility and tends to replay situations and life events over and over again in the mind instead of moving forward. The neurotic's self-talk becomes overly harsh and judgmental with an extraordinary amount of time spent on the past rather than the present.

In comparison, the character disorder is a personality type in which *no responsibility* is taken for behavior. It blames others for personal shortcomings and isn't accountable for decisions. Dr. Peck calls it an "escape from freedom."

According to Peck, "Whenever we seek to avoid the responsibility for our own behavior, we do so by attempting to give that responsibility to some other individual or organization or entity."[14] Character disorder personalities escape from freedom by blaming other people or circumstances for the problems they encounter. All of us seek to give up personal responsibility from time to time. The key is to become aware of this tendency and to stop this mode of thinking.

Some people go their whole lives stuck in a dependence mentality without ever knowing it. They wait for the promotion and complain about the status quo. On the other hand, the people who achieve significant success live by the credo, "If it's going to be, it's up to me." They recognize

[14] Peck, *The Road Less Traveled*, pg. 42.

it's their responsibility to make things happen. They find that their behavior promotes positive results both internally and externally.

Challenging Transition

Several years ago, I struggled with balancing personal responsibility and expectation as I transitioned back into banking after spending six years in the healthcare industry, including serving as CFO of a start-up company I formed with three classmates from business school. The return to banking was more difficult than I expected. I had to relearn many aspects of the job and my network of relationships and contacts was quite cold. I got my share of opportunities, but my batting average was terrible. At my low point I worked on eight deals in a row without landing one. I was exhausted and frustrated. Even worse, I began to question my abilities.

As I look back on it now, I had unrealistic expectations. In banking, or any complicated sales endeavor, winning business takes time, personal relationships, and trust. It resembles the growing cycle in farming discussed earlier, but it takes years rather than months.

Year One is the planting season. You meet people and companies, understand your market segment, and begin to make internal and external connections for later use. Year Two is the growing season. You grow relationships by bringing interesting ideas to the table, making introductions to relevant product experts, all the while building credibility with clients and prospects. Year Three is a time of harvest. You never harvest all the seeds you sow. However, those you do harvest often yield more than you ever thought possible. Your effort, knowledge, and credibility can now be used to win business that just a couple of years earlier would have been impossible.

This new way of thinking about my position was a breakthrough. I no longer blamed myself for lack of skill or ability; rather, I began to see the sales cycle as it really was—long. As a result, I brought a new attitude to work, and coupled with knowledge of the sales cycle, it led to substantial success. I stopped pressing so hard on each deal and focused on doing the things I needed to do in order to win business without a feeling of attachment to any one opportunity. I became more relaxed, trusting that the natural cycle would allow me to win business over time, and the change in demeanor came across as a quiet confidence that allowed the business to come naturally rather than as a forced result.

This transition back into banking was quite difficult and often humbling. However, it was vital that I learn from my mistakes and take a fresh look at my expectations. There were a whole host of situations, people, and bad luck available to take the blame for my failures, but I needed to not look for scapegoats and take positive steps toward finding solutions.

Guiding Principles

Personal responsibility is difficult to handle without a set of guiding principles to act as a compass on life's journey. It's not enough to know our strengths and intrinsic value as discussed earlier in the book. We need to take those strengths and develop our core guiding principles. Developing these involves a rigorous process of reflection and complete honesty. This process is difficult, rewarding, and necessary to guide us through life's challenges.

Establishing guiding principles is similar to creating a personal mission statement. The overarching goal is to begin making daily small decisions on the basis of our guiding principles. When we do, we begin to experience inner peace. Everyone wants inner peace, but until we begin to live in complete harmony with our guiding principles, such peace is elusive.

The following process of identifying our gifts and guiding principles is adapted from works by Laurie Beth Jones and Richard Leider.

Step One: Separate parents' principles from our own

Our strengths (gifts) will be a driver for the formation and development of our guiding principles. It's vital, however, to make certain we're not substituting the missed goals and regrets of our parents for our guiding principles. All of us have regrets for things done and things never done in life. Parents will often transfer these unfulfilled dreams to their children. Most of the time, neither the parent nor the child realizes this transference is taking place. We need to spend time thinking about what our parents' unfulfilled hopes and dreams were and are in order to guard ourselves against becoming prisoners to their principles.

First, start with the parent that had the most influence on you growing up. For me it was my dad. We were close from a very young age and he has had a profound influence on who I am today. In many respects he was an excellent role model. He worked hard, invested time with the family, and was a great sounding board whenever I needed help.

My dad was a business professor and he felt very strongly that getting a business degree was one of the best ways to prepare for a career after college. I took business courses at Furman University and even became president of the Association of Business Students to set myself apart upon graduation. During my senior year, I utilized the career placement office and interviewed with many companies, including three banks. Dad started his career in banking and felt this was an excellent career path:

Do you see where this is going? I'm not alone here. How many multi-generational lawyers, bankers, doctors, police officers, pharmacists, and small business owners are there in this country? There is absolutely nothing wrong with choosing a vocation that your father or mother spent their careers pursuing; however, it may not be your destiny. Likewise, many parents influence their children to pursue careers they never did and felt personal regret for that choice. Yet, it may not be in sync with our core strengths or guiding principles.

After my father began his career in banking, he left to go back to graduate school. He went on to complete his doctorate and began his career as a college professor. When I was a teenager, he left teaching to be a consultant. He was an outplacement consultant (career coach) during the massive layoffs of the 1980s and when that business dried up, he went back to teaching. The more I thought about it, the more I realized that my father's unfulfilled dream was becoming a successful executive. The primary measurement for success was how much money you made. He had transferred that dream so effectively over to me that it became my dream. But was it really my dream?

My mom's unmet dreams had to do with her strong need for love and approval. She is so kind and giving, and yet so insecure and fearful. I think her unmet dreams had more to do with being rescued and living a life of complete love and security. She was a very protective and loving mother. Ultimately, she never had enough faith and confidence in herself to be completely independent and she desperately desires that her children never feel similarly trapped in their lives.

Parents' Unmet Dreams:

Father: Successful executive (measured by wealth)

Mother: Cinderella (love and be loved)

Effect of Unmet Dreams:

Father: Emphasis on financial and business success

Mother: Too concerned with being liked and fearful of other's motives

Next, think about your parent's gifts and how they affect you:

Father: Teaching, leadership, logical thinking, work ethic

Mother: Thoughtfulness, caring, sensitivity, giving

If neither your mother nor father had a meaningful impact or influence on who you are today, think of others: uncle, grandmother, sibling, or even friends. The good news is that this type of reflection can work regardless of who had the most impact. The goal is to be open to your gifts and desires.

Next, think about your gifts and strengths as outlined in the strength inventory. Here are my strengths:

- I am disciplined
- I have a knowledge and passion for cars
- I am diplomatic
- I am loyal
- I am positive
- I am a good listener
- I am funny
- I lead by example
- I am a good coach
- I am sensitive to others' needs
- I motivate people to be their best
- I believe in servant leadership
- I am a hard worker
- I am constantly looking for ways to improve myself
- I am curious about the world around me
- I am a spiritual being
- I am fair

I realize there are people out there (especially my family) who might take issue with some of these strengths. I readily admit that I'm a work in progress and some of these strengths are not fully developed. However, my goal is to align these strengths with my daily activities in ways that build them into lasting gifts I can use as a basis for my guiding principles.

Step Two: Develop guiding principles

These principles should be a force in how we live no matter what vocation, life stage, or situation we find ourselves in. This unchanging core of who we are will provide us a sense of purpose and meaning whether we're in good times or adrift in a sea of challenges. These guiding principles represent our personal truth. My guiding principles are:

1. Seek spiritual connection in all aspects of life
2. Give maximum effort in all endeavors
3. Offer kindness and genuine interest in people
4. Practice honesty and integrity of thought and deed
5. Proactively handle conflict: stand up for my beliefs

These guiding principles were developed after spending a significant amount of time reflecting on who I am and who I strive to be. Furthermore, I find I experience the most peace and personal satisfaction when I act in concert with my guiding principles. Even though I've committed these guiding principles to memory, I find it helpful to keep a copy in my wallet. I refer to these core principles in times of stress or when I'm waiting for an airplane. They keep me focused on the things most important to me.

Insert your guiding principles into your daily life.

Step Three: Live your guiding principles

None of these principles would prevent me from being a banker. In fact, these principles would fit with a multitude of professions. The challenge in living our guiding principles is to insert them into our everyday lives. Without taking that step, they will ring hollow and our efforts in life will feel meaningless. For example, principle three is about my interest in giving myself to others. This takes many different forms including teaching, mentoring, coaching, and charity work. Fulfilling this guiding principle means much more to me than just being nice to colleagues at work or strangers in a grocery store. I needed to do more than these things to live in sync with this principle and, as a result, I felt a deep sense of regret. I was not living in sync with one of my core principles.

I began slowly to change my actions in order to fulfill this area of principal importance. It began with my son Jack's baseball team. I didn't play baseball growing up, but I had developed a great interest in it while living in Atlanta and following the Braves. Jack loved playing baseball and I was an assistant coach for a number of seasons before working up the courage to be a head coach. I had a lot of excuses: no prior playing or coaching experience and a job with travel. But it was nine-year-old baseball; surely I could handle this challenge! I found the reward to be so much greater than what I'd expected and experienced so much joy in motivating and encouraging the boys. I took so much pride in seeing improvement in skills and teamwork through the season. It was a wonderful!

Baseball was just the beginning; I was also determined to expand my efforts around guiding principle one. I really desired a closer relationship with God. Neither Kim nor I were attending church regularly and yet both of our children were in weekly Sunday school classes in preparation for first communion and confirmation. I felt like a hypocrite. We made up our minds that attending church was going to become a priority. We started going to church each week in 2007 and the ties we have developed through church have been meaningful for the whole family.

I began looking for something more and signed up for church retreats. The first retreat I went on was a workshop on what it means to be a male Christian. It was a great educational experience, but I realized it was only the beginning at church. I'm now learning how to be a more generous person, both with my time and my money. I'm expanding my life in areas that are extremely exciting and rewarding and this change is a product of living my guiding principles. That being said, I have a long way to go. I'm barely scratching the surface.

These are just a few tangible ways I've been able to incorporate my guiding principles into my everyday life. I've found a greater peace knowing I'm living in accordance with a moral compass developed by me, for me. This process can have the same result for your personal life. Don't push these feelings away! The goal of this book is to get us back to the core of who we are—described in the first chapter as the Natural Self.

Free Agent

Have you ever envied the free agents in professional sports? Each sport has different rules about qualifying for free agency, but the principle is the same. Once players reach a specific tenure, they qualify for free agency. Free agency allows them to play for the team that provides the best terms of employment. Since professional sports careers are very short compared with most vocations, players tend to go with teams that pay the most money. Free agency is the ultimate goal of pro athletes because it allows them to take control of their careers and maximize their income.

We're free agents too, but our free agency is far easier to achieve than the free agency in professional sports. We're free agents in the game of life. Even though the rules are not as explicit in most careers compared with professional sports regarding skills, years of service, and experience, we're free agents when finding the jobs that best match our needs. In other words, we're ultimately responsible for our career or vocation.

My father took the free agent concept to the extreme with many job changes, both within academia and as a consultant. He looks back and regrets some of the moves as being impetuous and not well thought out; however, he takes full responsibility for these free agency moves. Even though the big contracts are what make the headlines in pro sports, in some cases, players are willing to take less for a longer contract or to stay with teams where they're comfortable. It's important to remember that we're ultimately responsible for our careers and the decisions we make. How are you performing as a free agent in the game of life?

Just because you and I don't have an agent negotiating multi-million dollar contracts on our behalf does not absolve our responsibility as free agents in our chosen careers. As such, we need to ask ourselves the following questions at least every three years.[15]

1. Am I working in a position and for a company that allows me to be in harmony with my guiding principles? If not, is it truly the job or is it how I am performing in that job?

2. Would additional education make a difference in my position and opportunity for advancement? Would other types of executive education assist me in attaining my goals?

3. Am I taking full advantage of the opportunities for career education and job change opportunities at work? Do I reach out to colleagues in other divisions within the company to build a network and identify potential areas of interest for my career path?

4. If this isn't my chosen vocation, am I doing all I can to transition into the job or field that is more in sync with my interests and guiding principles? Am I taking full advantage of free agency?

The answers to these questions will guide you along the path of personal responsibility, toward the right career fit for you. Ultimately, it's up to you whether or not you actually embrace the spirit and responsibility of being a free agent and act on your core beliefs.

Bloom Where You're Planted

Miracles surround us in everyday life, but it's our responsibility to find the good where there is bad, or to give our best when we're

[15] My father and I co-authored a book titled *Career PREParation, A Transition Guide for Students* (New Jersey: Pearson Prentice Hall, 2004), which provides a step-by-step guide to seeking and obtaining a profession given your skills and interests.

feeling our worst. Although we'll discuss life's miracles and guideposts from God in more detail later in the book, let's begin now by taking a walk outside and observing the small things we routinely overlook right where we live. In particular, seek out signs of life in improbable places. Do you see a flower growing in a crack in the sidewalk? How about the tree that grows through a jumble of rocks in an abandoned lot? What about the bird's nest precariously built on the side of an abandoned shed?

When I was in my twenties, I traveled the "17-mile drive" on the Monterey coast. This is a spectacular drive past some of Northern California's most photographed sites such as Pebble Beach, Seal Rock, and Monterey Bay. One of the most beautiful vistas on the entire drive, however, is a simple, lone cypress. You have probably seen the pictures, but pictures cannot duplicate seeing The Lone Cypress in person. Here is a tree improbably growing out of a rugged outcropping of rocks high above Monterey Bay, and it defies explanation. It's at once both majestic and fragile. It inspires thousands to take its picture with a beauty and grace that touches the hearts of those who see it. Its beauty lies in its tenacious grip on life despite the circumstances.

Why is one tree able to grow out of a rock when other trees nearby with an abundance of soil, sun, and water languish? Like the cypress, we're called to bloom and be fruitful no matter where we're planted. This is where personal responsibility must transcend our own life situation. Each of us is ultimately recognized for how we bloom or bear fruit regardless of our current or past life story. Some people are able to bear fruit under the most difficult of circumstances while others are bitter and negative despite wealth and numerous other advantages.

Personal responsibility is best revealed when we're placed in the most difficult of circumstances. There are times we find ourselves in a job or life situation we never imagined and it's difficult to get up in the morning and do the most basic of tasks. In order to bloom here, we must first accept our situation. Although this might sound counter-intuitive, acceptance is the starting point of personal responsibility. A period of time is usually needed to properly evaluate where we are now and what direction we desire our life's journey to take next. Once we accept our current situation, we're ready to take responsibility for affecting change. Most difficult circumstances or "dead ends" were not created overnight; therefore, it will take time, effort, and discipline to create positive results.

One of the best ways to speed the process out of negativity and into positive momentum is through a proper attitude. When we become a blessing to others (blooming) regardless of our personal situation (where we are planted today), we open ourselves up to coincidence and serendipity—life's everyday miracles. Each of us is called by God to bear good fruit. We do this in numerous ways: helping a sick neighbor, volunteering at church, coaching our child's soccer team. Once we become responsible for where we are on life's path, it becomes easier to be more fruitful in all we do.

Take responsibility now for your blooms of positive attitude and inspire those around you to share the spirit of peace and happiness.

Key Takeaways:

1. There are two personality types: the neurotic and the character disorder. The neurotic takes on too much responsibility for negative life events. The character disorder personality does not take responsibility for his actions or place in life.

2. "Escape from freedom" is when we blame events or individuals for our current life situation. We escape from freedom when we do not take responsibility for our lives.

3. God helps those who help themselves—the key is to move forward in faith.

4. Developing our guiding principles will align our internal with our external goals.

5. We must orient our work and personal life to be consistent with our guiding principles in order to experience peace and happiness.

6. It's vital to insert our guiding principles into our daily lives.

7. We're all free agents in the game of life; therefore, we must take control of our work life to be more in sync with our guiding principles.

8. There are times when we must make the best out of difficult circumstances. No matter what our life story, we're called to bloom where we're planted.

9. When we sow seeds of bitterness and negativity, we will harvest the same in our lives.

10. When we give what we want to receive we will receive back more abundantly than we ever imagined.

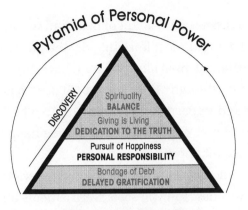

Pyramid of Personal Power

DISCOVERY

Spirituality
BALANCE

Giving is Living
DEDICATION TO THE TRUTH

Pursuit of Happiness
PERSONAL RESPONSIBILITY

Bondage of Debt
DELAYED GRATIFICATION

CHAPTER 5

THE PURSUIT OF HAPPINESS

"We hold these truths to be self-evident, that all men are created equal,
that they are endowed by their Creator with certain unalienable Rights,
that among these are Life, Liberty, and the pursuit of Happiness."
– Thomas Jefferson

The second line of the Declaration of Independence is one of the most famous sentences ever written. It's a beautiful line that should be an inspiration to all of us who live in the United States and who may take for granted the freedom and liberties we have as a people. Many scholars have spent entire careers focused on the beautiful and meaningful words of the Declaration of Independence since it's the foundation on which our country's constitution was built. At its core, *it underscores that each person has innate value bestowed upon them by their Creator.* It emphasizes the value of the individual as part of the whole.

Although the Declaration is full of beautiful writing and insightful truths, the phrase I find most intriguing is "the *pursuit* of Happiness." It emphasizes that all men and women have the right to pursue happiness. Even though the United States has its share of discrimination and imperfection, I know of no other country where the citizens have better opportunities to pursue happiness. Then why are so many of us unhappy?

All you have to do is spend an hour watching television to understand what our society values. You will see advertisements for new cars, new clothes, and all manner of products designed to make us look more youthful, more desirable. We build big houses with big loans as the material symbol of the "Good Life." From the moment we enter the workforce until we reach our forties, many of us consider this accumulation of bigger, better, and nicer as all part of the pursuit of happiness. However, the accumulation of possessions is the "fool's gold" of happiness.

This outward pursuit cannot satisfy our need for inner peace and happiness. If all we do is pursue the outward, material forms of happiness, we'll never find it. As we discussed earlier, these cravings are part of an insatiable hunger that feeds the Treadmill Effect.

Are we relying on someone or something to determine our happiness? Do we think we'll only be happy after we achieve that next, external goal? Do we find ourselves dreaming about finishing this sentence: "I will finally be happy when _____?" The good news is we can break this cycle of seeking happiness in people or things. It may take a little time and faith, depending on how deeply these habits are entrenched, but we can set ourselves free from the folly of mining fool's gold.

The Treasure Within

Paulo Coelho wrote a parable that underscores the importance of following our dreams and guiding principles, or as he puts it, our "personal legend." In his book *The Alchemist*, Santiago, a poor shepherd boy has a heart full of big dreams. His quest for discovery of his unique and guiding principles is full of ups and downs, self-doubt, and disappointment, yet ultimately, his faith conquers his fears.

Along the way, he finds he has the talent to sell fine china and crystal, and in time, he makes a great deal of money for himself and the local store owner who has lost his desire to pursue his own personal legend. At this point, and at several other instances along the way, Santiago nearly gives up. However, he presses on in faith and seems guided by a spiritual intelligence and wisdom far beyond that of a youth. I won't give away the ending, but the poor shepherd boy discovers his outward treasure only after he discovers the treasure within.

Like Santiago, we all have a treasure within that will only be discovered by pursuing a life dedicated to our unique gifts and guiding principles. There is an internal battle being fought in each one of us for our faith, love, and destiny. I believe we're living to discover or *remember* our true calling. I say remember because many of us know implicitly or subconsciously what we should be doing in life, the pursuit of which will bring happiness and fulfillment.

Think back to your childhood. What were you like? What was your passion? Remember some of the things you did that resulted in absolute focus. These are the activities that give us glimpses of our true selves: who we are, what we love, and where our true passions lie. In many cases, these moments occurred when we were young and had not yet encountered many of the slings and arrows of life that resulted in cynicism and closed our hearts. Our goal as adults should be to evaluate ourselves honestly so as to become self-aware of our unique gifts, and then to pursue a life in sync with these truths. Peace, love and happiness are all characteristics that are present when we're living consistently with our guiding principles.

Eliminate and Facilitate

In order to eliminate bad habits, we need to replace them with good ones. The eliminate-and-facilitate process is easy in principle, but it takes awareness, will, and effort to change behavior. It has transformed my life and given me an incredible amount of happiness, peace, and joy. It can do the same for you.

The process starts by eliminating roadblocks to happiness.

Roadblocks to happiness are everywhere and nowhere. That is to say, we will encounter many issues daily—some small and some large—that will test us. Our patience is tested as we drive to work, help with our children's homework, and handle an angry client or co-worker. Our peace is tested when we work with someone who constantly complains. Our faith is tested when we encounter a serious health issue with a family member or friend. How we handle these challenges will largely determine how happy we are. In other words, it's not the event that steals our happiness, but our reaction to that event. As Abraham Lincoln said, "Most folks are about as happy as they make up their minds to be."

In addition to roadblocks, there are potholes on the path to happiness. What about "Life's Little Annoyances?" How do we handle the traffic jam or the series of red lights we encounter? If we tense up and lash out at how unfair the situation is, we bring undue stress into our lives. This is the principle discussed earlier in the book about stimulus and response. Ultimately, each one of us is responsible for our responses to these stimuli. We can either tie ourselves up in knots or we can let it go and release it.

"Tis nothing either good or bad, but thinking makes it so."
Hamlet – William Shakespeare

The first step in eliminating happiness roadblocks or potholes is to be aware of our annoyances. Many of us are blind to our hang-ups unless we really spend time thinking about them. The next step is to write these little annoyances down and reflect on them. Are they really important? Is there a way to avoid the situation that brings them on? This is my list of annoyances:

- A long commute filled with stop-and-go traffic
- Waiting more than ten minutes to be seated at a restaurant
- Waiting in check-out lines
- Being stuck in traffic upon leaving a sporting event
- A discourteous sales person or poor service at a restaurant
- Thoughtless or selfish behavior at work or in the community
- Children whining or complaining about chores, schoolwork, etc.
- Children not cleaning up after themselves

If I were to compare my list with yours, I suspect there would be many common themes; however, one thing particularly stands out on nearly everyone's list. With most of the small issues that annoy us, *we have no immediate control except over our reaction to that annoyance.* Remember, control is a big factor in happiness. When we don't feel in control of our lives or our emotions, we become very unhappy. Our only control when confronting these small annoyances is how we react to them.

For each item on the list, determine whether or not you have control over the annoyance. In the first example, "a long commute filled with stop-and-go traffic," you have limited control on any given day, but you do have control over that annoyance over time. You can move closer to your job, you can change jobs, or you can ask your employer for a non-traditional work schedule (get in early and leave early). Therefore, you recognize that you do have some degree of control over this situation in the longer term. Get to work on those items if this is an issue that truly impacts your enjoyment in life. However, in the short run, recognize that you have very limited control over this situation. In my case, I take a deep breath, let it out, and consciously make the decision not to allow this to be a stress event in my life. I either meditate or listen to an audio book on my MP3 player—I try to keep a good supply of these ready. I take control over my response to this annoyance and realize that my reaction is completely my responsibility.

Once we take the step of thinking about (or *becoming conscious of*) those small things that bring a level of stress and annoyance into our lives, we put ourselves in a position to control our negative reactions. Many of us do not take this step and remain blind to these roadblocks to happiness. Negative emotional reactions will spring from out of nowhere and we begin to feel powerless in our own lives. The awareness of these triggers place us back in control. Life is too wonderful to get caught up in the negativity that these small hang-ups bring. Be responsible for changing your response to these frustrations and you will find yourself much happier.

Break the Fear and Worry Habit

I graduated with an MBA in 1997 and made the decision to go into business with two other classmates. I was twenty-nine years old and this was a big decision for me. Up to this point, my career had been spent working for a large bank, and even though I was looking for a change, a certain amount of security and familiarity was tied to that position that I would be giving up in this new venture.

The next three years were the most challenging, stress-filled years of my life. We were successful in raising the capital needed to build three locations (Atlanta, Nashville, and Las Vegas). However, each day brought an unending flow of new situations that I had never confronted before. I was both CFO and VP of Development. The CFO role was not such a big departure from my experience as a banker. But my development role meant that I was responsible for hiring and managing a sales force, developing marketing materials, and speaking

CHAPTER 5 – THE PURSUIT OF HAPPINESS

to large groups of insurance brokers to introduce our service offering. I was over my head and felt like I was sinking fast.

Over time, the stress level climbed higher as we tried to get our facilities to break even. Each of us guaranteed a substantial amount of debt that had been used to fund our start-up costs and the situation was pretty dire. My bank training took over and I began exploring downside scenarios at partner meetings. I remember thinking at the time that the founding partner Dr. P seemed very calm and almost oblivious to the dire situation. I asked the question that was on everybody's mind, "Aren't you concerned about our situation? Why aren't you giving us your thoughts on these scenarios?" I remember him looking me straight in the eye and saying, "Dave, worry is a misuse of imagination. I don't see these as negatives that can't be overcome." He was as cool as a cucumber and I was stunned at what I felt was his reckless disregard of the situation. The business he had founded was a train heading toward a cliff of failure and he was talking about opportunity. Who was this guy—Peter Pan?

Worry is a misuse of imagination.

As it turned out, I had reason to be worried. We were burning through cash faster than we were able to bring our facilities to break-even. Despite our best efforts to raise capital and buy ourselves more time, we ultimately were forced to cut the staff dramatically (including me and my other partner) and eventually the business was sold to another company for a price far less than valuations just nine months earlier. In the aftermath of this less-than-successful entrepreneurial experience, I did a lot of soul-searching. Why was I so worried while Dr. P was unfazed by what occurred? Who was less rational, me or him? Did I truly have, "a reason to be worried" or did my worry become a self-fulfilling prophecy?

As I looked back on those three years, I realized that they were filled with a high level of stress that was brought about by constant worry. Don't get me wrong; there were critical issues to worry about. However, worrying was not going to help us solve our problems. I needed to look more deeply into what had become such beacons for worry.

Combating a Deadly Enemy

Worry is deadly for three reasons. First, it's a negative preoccupation on the future instead of a laser focus on what's in front of us today. Ultimately, executing our business plan today was the only thing we had control over. When our minds are cluttered by "what if" worries, we have a difficult time focusing on the matter at hand; being creative; and problem solving.

Second, a constant preoccupation with the downside has a way of giving possibility to downside results that may never have happened otherwise. We're free to choose what we think about all day long, and we must choose to use our imaginations to create good rather than worry about the negative; otherwise, we may find that our worst worries come true.

"A man is what he thinks about all day long." – Ralph Waldo Emerson

---

Third, constant worry is much like having a chronic health problem. It saps our joy and often brings with it a cloud of depression. If left unchecked for a long period, high levels of stress often bring on serious health problems. Our minds and bodies are inextricably linked and constant stress in one area (significant worry) can bring about very real health problems such as high blood pressure, shortness of breath, and even cancer.

So how do we turn this negative spiral of emotions upside down into something more positive? In my own life, when I find myself worrying about the future, I discipline myself to take the following steps.

Step One: Make peace with the worst-case scenario—today!

Before embarking on a new venture or challenge, consider the downside of doing poorly or failing altogether. I know this might sound a little strange; almost as if we're setting ourselves up for failure, but in most cases just the opposite happens. When we sit down and truly consider the implications for failure, we usually find that the fear of failure is far greater than the actual failure itself.

Ask yourself, "What's the worst thing that could happen if I failed at this?" If you cannot accept the worst-case scenario, you should strongly consider not embarking on the venture. If you find that you're making this choice over and over again, you may have a totally different problem in which you lack confidence in yourself to move forward in life, to evolve and improve.

In my case, the downside scenario came true. Newco was not able to reach the break-even point. I had to rethink the next steps in my career, and get a new job. I only had one child at the time, Kim was still working at the bank, and I had time to find something else. The downside really wasn't that bad, as I could have always returned to banking (which I eventually did). Because I never took the time on the front end to consider the worst-case scenario and make peace with it, fear of failure was worse than the reality. Think about how my performance would have improved if I had done so. Rather than feeling a chronic level of stress brought on by what the future might hold, I would have been more focused and solutions oriented.

Step Two: Maximize effort

When we're embarking on something new, it's vital that we give our best effort. We never want to look back at a failed project, venture, or challenge and know in our hearts that we did not give our very best effort. On the other hand, we can't beat ourselves up for making mistakes. Experience comes the hard way; we learn from our mistakes. We must recognize that in order to have peace we must believe that we gave our best effort regardless of the outcome.

There's a term in tennis for not giving your very best. It's called "tanking" a match. The worst thing you can say about a competitor is that he or she tanked a match or game. Athletes can actually get fined for not giving their best effort. Even so, the individual who tanks is hurt the most.

We've all been in situations where we're completely spent, unmotivated, or negative about a given activity. Giving our best effort in these situations builds character and integrity. No one is going to have a perfect record, but it's so important to give our best on a consistent basis; to cultivate a habit of excellence, if you will. One of my guiding principles highlights this fact: "Maximum effort in all endeavors."

Am I perfect? Ask Kim how I throw myself into washing the dishes or cleaning up after myself. I have a long way to go, but I'm committed to giving my best!

Step Three: Success comes from failure

The American spirit of hard work, rugged individualism, and responsibility is admired the world over. Men and women are celebrated when they beat tremendous odds to succeed in a particular endeavor. But what about the flipside—failure? Many of the stories celebrating success don't tell the story of the failures leading to that ultimate success. It's as though these people were pre-ordained to succeed without ever experiencing the challenges and frustration of failure. Conversely, think about the many stories of failure. The news media has a morbid fascination with failure regarding sports, movies, or business.

We've all felt the sting of failure, but it has such a negative stigma in our society that many people are afraid to take the risks needed to win. I'm convinced that those willing to risk failure have a healthy self-concept. They realize that failure is merely a detour on the road to success. I admire those who are willing to risk failure because they believe in something; they are passionate about their vocation and are willing to risk failure to achieve success. A key way to eliminate worry and fear is to gain a key perspective on failure. And that is simply this: we only achieve success through failure.

IMMUTABLE LAW 5
We only achieve success through failure.

Show me any successful person you want, and I will show you someone who failed multiple times before becoming successful. Once we truly believe and internalize this fact, we realize that the only way we can become successful is through failure. This is a universal truth, an immutable law that cannot be changed. From our earliest days of learning to walk and talk, read and write; we met success only after experiencing failure. This is known as experiential learning and is the most natural way for humans to learn.

As kids, we're free to fail and repeat multiple times with our parents as watchful supporters, encouraging us along the way. The stakes are low and the rewards are high; as a result, we're learning machines. As we grow into young adults, the perceived stakes become higher as our peers and society judge what we do as either successful or not. However, the natural law of success through failure does not change just because we become more self-conscious of our failures.

Therefore, it is those willing to conquer fear of failure who ultimately find the best success in life. Fear prevents us from becoming all that we can be in our chosen vocation and life in general.

A newspaper reporter interviewed Thomas Edison and asked him how he was able to keep going after failing so many times before perfecting the light bulb. Edison didn't miss a beat in his reply and said, "I have not failed. I've just found 10,000 ways that won't work."

"I have not failed. I've just found 10,000 ways that won't work."
— Thomas Edison

Once we realize success ultimately comes from failure, we take the teeth out of the shark of failure. It's not such a scary creature anymore. Experience builds over time and that confidence allows us to focus more on the job at hand and less on fears and worries of failure.

These steps, when used properly, can reduce worry and anxiety. And when we remove worry, we find a renewed peace and joy in living. The more we're able to focus on the present, the better equipped we are to succeed.

Uprooting Bitterness with Forgiveness

The slings and arrows of life can cause us to hide our hearts behind a thick wall of protection. We effectively put on a mask for the world while struggling internally with our demons. If we aren't careful, these hurts, challenges, or injustices may result in discouragement, frustration, and even bitterness, which is the most damaging of these emotions. Bitterness is defined as a feeling of deep resentment, anger, and ill-will.

How many times has something unfair happened to us and we replay the scene over and over in our heads. The more we think about it, the more hurt, upset, or even enraged we become. When we walk around with these emotions, we bring a negative attitude to all we face and happiness becomes a distant memory. It's as though a dark cloud (our negative feelings) follows us around and colors all our experiences.

Bitterness is often addressed in the New and Old Testaments of the Bible. Hebrews 12:15 (NIV) says, "See to it that no one misses the grace of God and that no bitter root grows up to cause trouble and defile many." The Scripture says the root of bitterness can cause us to become diseased, polluted, or filthy. When we think bad or negative thoughts, they can pollute us. In order to obtain God's best gifts and graces, we cannot have this bitter root in our lives.

"See to it that no one misses the grace of God and that no bitter root grows up to cause trouble and defile many."
– Hebrews 12:15 (NIV)

At its core, bitterness is an emotion borne out of a lack of control in our thinking, and when left unchecked, it becomes a root that grows inside of us. When we carry bitterness, it's impossible to focus on the present. Think of it as the root of an unwanted weed or vine; instead of bearing the fruit of happiness, peace, and satisfaction, it produces anger, malice, and resentment. This root is insatiable, meaning the more we feed it, the more it wants from us. If left unchecked, it will consume our thinking, our energy, and our ability to focus on the various issues of the day. Taken to its extreme, the root of bitterness can become debilitating and all-consuming. People have been known to throw away families and careers, all in the name of a consuming bitterness.

The wise person realizes that he or she has control over negative emotions, and that control is found in the act of forgiveness. Forgiveness is one of the most difficult things we will ever do. We may know from our upbringing that forgiveness is the right thing to do, but in practice, it is extraordinarily challenging. It takes a leap of faith because our Judging Minds have already found the person guilty as charged.

Think about someone in your life who has done something to you that is "unforgivable." When you think about that person, what comes to mind? Do you hope ill-will and even violence against that person? If so, you have not completely forgiven that person and a root of bitterness still grows inside you. Forgiveness is for the forgiver not the forgiven. Do you think that person gives you a second thought? Do you think he or she even remembers what they did to you in the first place that caused you so much pain? Probably not.

We need to forgive others so we may be at peace with ourselves. We need forgiveness to regain control of our emotions. Only through forgiveness are we able to remove bitterness from our hearts and move forward in peace and love. The act of forgiveness is when we're closest to God, because it transcends the Judging Mind with an act of grace.

Forgiveness of the past allows us to be fully aware of and engaged in the present. Think about how good you feel when you clean out the clutter in your house or garage. Similarly, mental clutter and clinging to the past have a way of holding us back from the wonderful world in the present. Forgiveness is the secret to sweeping away negative mental clutter. Allow forgiveness to bring freedom and happiness into your life.

Positive Expectations

It's absolutely true that, over time, we bring about the expectations we have in our heart. As a result, there is a practical reason for positive expectations in what we do. To the extent we believe in our ability to succeed, we will indeed succeed over time. However, the flipside is also true. If we believe we do not have what it takes to succeed, we'll likely fail.

Over the long term, we attract the people and situations into our lives that resonate with the core of our personal beliefs and desires. This should be an empowering realization for all of us who have a deep desire for developing our personal success and fully realizing our personal mission. It's vital that we train our minds to think and act positively. Positive expectations help us rebound more quickly when events in life do not go our way.

There's a big difference between intellectually understanding that positive expectations are manifested over time and actually practicing this law of positive attraction. The older we get the more painful failure becomes. It's human nature to avoid pain, and failure is a painful event. Our minds are programmed to protect us from failure by reminding us of those situations in which we have experienced failure. However, we must push through these uncomfortable feelings if we are to grow and to progress. We must recognize that failure through experiential learning is our only pathway toward successful results. It's extremely difficult for most of us to believe this "faith in failure" and maintain our positive expectations. Our minds are so judgmental that we condemn our actions and become reluctant to try again.

Let's revisit a book I quoted in Chapter One. In *Release Your Brakes*, James Newman used the term "comfort zone." Our comfort zone acts as our "effectiveness regulator" which means that over time, our effectiveness will be limited to where we feel most comfortable. He states:

The Effectiveness Regulator concept helps to explain why "will power" is so ineffective and sometimes destructive. Will power is the teeth-gritting, fist-clenching, determined effort to change one's behavior—the deliberate, conscious attempt to move outside the Comfort Zone. Of course it is possible to do that. You do have the capacity to act in a manner that is not "like you." But the tension that kind of action produces within your system is very uncomfortable, and the net result of the self-talk which is stimulated by that discomfort will probably be to lower the self-image setting on the *Regulator*.[16]

According to Newman, the only way we're able to break out of our narrow comfort zone is to change the setting of our effectiveness regulator by doing these new activities over and over again in our minds until we master them and no longer perceive them as being outside of our comfort zone. He uses a process of "constructive imagination" or what I referred to earlier as visualization, to practice these events until we feel more positive about our abilities in a given discipline. For example, the individual who wants to improve her public speaking skills would imagine getting up in front of a group visibly confident in herself and the material. She would imagine engaging the audience with ease and the positive feelings that would be part of such a presentation. The key, according to Newman, is to experience the activity in the first person. In other words, we should not be a spectator watching ourselves, but the actual deliverer of the presentation as this process will reinforce the actual behavior as though we actually delivered the speech.

There's no question that visualization will enhance our ability to become more comfortable in a given task. It will help us deal with our mind's reluctance to place us in a situation where failure is a possibility. It's a practical way to build positive expectations into our life experiences that will greatly enhance our attitude when taking on a new challenge. However, visualization must be used in concert with the actual activity in order to make the most progress. I can visualize my tennis stroke repeatedly, but without going to the court and building the muscle memory of my new and improved groundstroke, it will be difficult to

---

[16] Newman, pg. 92.

make lasting improvements. The same is true in any area of life in which we want to make real and lasting improvements. Utilize visualization or constructive imagination to help build confidence, but reinforce that visualization by doing. We'll find that both activities will yield more positive results through our positive expectations.

Quiet the Mind

We're a nation of doers and we have an almost unlimited number of activities and distractions that keep us busy. Way too busy! On the cover of our children's school activity calendar is the phrase "Endless Possibilities." Both my wife and I know this fact all too well as we attempt to manage our own calendars to participate in many of these school, recreational, and sports activities. In addition to school programs, we both participate in church activities and attend occasional community benefits, which all add up to a very full calendar.

Setting aside time for our own relationship is a challenge. We're fortunate to have my mom in town, which allows some date nights and weekend getaways, but these times are few and far between. Also, these rare times out together do not train us how to quiet the mind and enjoy our present moment. We often find ourselves talking about the next game, the next event, or past challenges at school or work.

When we become exceedingly busy, it becomes exceedingly difficult to enjoy the present moment. How tough is it in your life to live the axiom, "Stop and smell the roses"? I find myself thinking about the most recent life event or future activity with very little thought of the present. This incessant worry about the past and concern about the future is the "noise" in our lives that prevents us from enjoying the present. John Lennon famously said it this way, "Life is what happens while you are busy making other plans."

"Life is what happens while you are busy making other plans."
– John Lennon

Why is this happening?

Because our minds become addicted to our activities, the ego or mind becomes wrapped up in the challenge and drama surrounding events in our lives. In many cases, the activities can become the ultimate distraction from the true dissatisfaction that may be present. We know deep down whether or not we are living in accordance with our guiding principles, but we refuse to allow quiet reflection. The noise of planning and living our lives in the past and future can become a distraction from the truly important things in life. Invariably, these distractions become an equally dissatisfying way of life.

When we become over-booked and over-stimulated, we begin to lose control of ourselves. An addiction is the ultimate lack of control. Ask yourself this simple question: "Am I in control of my life or am I living out the addictions of my mind?" More often than not, our mind addictions are dominated by desires for material things such as a new dress, house, car, or furniture. Having goals that allow us to attain material goods isn't a bad thing, but it cannot be the only thing. Remember, no matter how much material wealth we attain, it can never bring us lasting peace and fulfillment. Only living in accordance with our guiding principles will bring us closer to our true selves and the comfort and peace that come with it.

In his bestselling book *The Power of Now*,[17] Eckhart Tolle delves deeply into the importance of the present moment. As he puts it, "There is no other moment other than the present moment." He encourages us to "live in the now" and eliminate the mind's preoccupation with past and future, as both are irrelevant and impediments to making the most of the present.

---

[17] Eckhart Tolle, The Power of Now: A Guide to Spiritual Enlightenment (Novato, New World Library, 2004), pg. 41.

So, how do we quiet the mind? Like any positive habit we want to develop, it takes focus and practice, but over time will pay big dividends. Here are three disciplines to start with:

1. *Meditate twice a day for at least ten minutes:*

Meditation is a way in which we listen to God and our innermost self. It's a valuable tool for quieting the mind. When you first begin practicing meditation, you may get discouraged as your busy mind jumps from one thought or topic to another. You shouldn't get frustrated but just return your mind from the passing thought to your breathing. In and out. Feel the rhythm of your breathing, your chest moving back and forth. If the thoughts are tough to control, you may find it helpful to say a phrase over and over again, such as "peace, love and happiness," or "trust in God." The goal is to quiet the Judging Mind for at least ten minutes twice a day.

2. *Take "Observation Gaps":*

Focus on a tree outside the window or a picture of your family. The goal isn't to think about the object or the picture but to quiet the mind, if only for a minute or two. Again, we're exercising control over our thinking and Judging Minds. This exercise is especially valuable when we have a problem and just can't figure out what to do. When we quiet the mind, the answer will many times bubble up from deep within without us even knowing we had the answer the whole time. The trick is in quieting the mind and allowing our subconscious to unlock the answer.

3. *Thankful prayer:*

Whenever we take time to thank God for our many gifts, we're reaffirming those gifts in our own minds. I know of people who take thankful prayer to the next level and write down all the good things that happened to them that day just before they go to bed. Our minds love to wrestle with problems, but we don't spend as much time reflecting on the gifts we have been given through little or no effort on our part. By spending time in thankful prayer and reflection on life's "daily miracles" we become much more relaxed and grateful.

Key Takeaways:
1. The Declaration of Independence emphasizes the value of the individual and the right each of us has to pursue happiness without a guarantee of the achievement of happiness.

2. The Eliminate-and-Facilitate system of happiness reduces our negative responses to life's challenges while amplifying the blessings in our lives that often go unnoticed.

3. Refuse to allow life's annoyances to bring you down. If you have control over the irritant, make a change. If you don't, make a habit of peaceful acceptance.

4. Break the fear and worry habit by developing a discipline around life's challenges. When we face a difficult challenge:
    a. understand and make peace with the worst-case scenario;
    b. learn what it takes to accomplish our goals and use maximum effort to achieve them;
    c. don't get discouraged by failure because it breeds success.

5. Whenever we cast a bright light on our fear, it begins to fade away.

6. Never allow a root of bitterness to grow within our hearts. True forgiveness frees us from bitterness. It lightens the heart

and allows us to appreciate all we have today without thoughts of bitterness from yesterday.

7. The Judging Mind is our harshest critic. The best way to control its damaging words is to consciously monitor our self-talk and to be a positive coach and mentor to ourselves.

8. Experiential learning is the best way to learn. Positive expectations result when we change our thinking about failure and recognize that practice allows us to achieve ultimate success.

9. We become happier and more at peace when we are able to focus on the present moment.

10. Utilize these tools to quiet the mind:
    a. meditate at least twice a day for ten minutes;
    b. take mini-breaks throughout the day to focus quietly on an object or your breathing;
    c. practice thankful prayer.

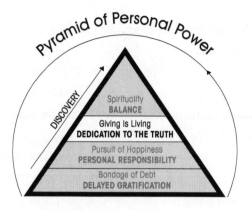

CHAPTER 6

DEDICATION
TO THE TRUTH

"Rather than love, than money, than fame, give me truth."
– Henry David Thoreau

A ccording to the Encarta World English Dictionary, truth is defined as, "Something factual: the thing that corresponds to fact or reality." However, words and definitions are mostly inadequate when discussing truth because it is at the heart of all we are and the creation that surrounds us. I believe truth is far greater than a dictionary definition. I define truth as, "The natural laws of the universe." Throughout this book I've highlighted "Immutable Laws," which could just as easily be called "Immutable Truths."

Whenever we violate a law or a truth, we violate the essence of who we are. It's when we're in violation of the truth, or the natural laws of the universe, that we become dissatisfied with life. When that happens, most of us don't realize we're in violation of the truth. Instead, we feel the world is against us.

In reality, this is our ego or Judging Mind lashing out. When we separate ourselves from the rest of the world by demanding to be treated better, differently, or fairly, we're really saying that our "Self Law" (or the laws of the Judging Mind) should supersede the natural laws of the universe. When our selfish desires are in conflict with the greater truth, life becomes a daily battle against the world and very difficult indeed. We view life as a zero-sum game in which more for my wife, brother, colleague, or neighbor becomes less for me. Rather than living with an abundance mentality, we live with a scarcity mentality. It's necessary, therefore, to become conscious of our thinking and behavior in order to realign with the Greater Truth.

When we become aware of the Judging Mind and how it removes us from the real world we can begin to align ourselves with the truth. Aligning with the truth is very simple, but also very difficult. Here's why. By aligning the truth, we subordinate the ego's desires. The ego does not like to have its will subordinated and it fights back. The will is difficult to overcome and it can never be silenced completely. However, our goal is to create gaps of awareness around the needs and desires of the ego so we may become more conscious of how it might obscure the natural laws of the universe. These gaps allow us to see the truth and achieve inner peace.

Jesus' teachings underscore this reality. In John 12:35 (NIV), Jesus says, "Walk while you have the light, before darkness overtakes you. The man who walks in the dark does not know where he is going." When he says "light," he is referring to truth. Only after we're able to understand what is true are we able to know where we're going. And when Jesus says, "I am the way and the truth and the life. No one comes to the Father except through me" (John 14:6, NIV), he is also talking about the truth. The peace of God only comes to those who subjugate their own desires and align themselves with the present reality or truth.

So what is his truth? Simply this: we should live our lives conscious of the fact that we are part of the larger whole. When we become aware of this, we'll be more generous and forgiving to our fellow man and the environment. We can tamp out the selfish wants of our Judging Minds and their unending desires of more.

A Liberal Arts Education

I attended a small liberal arts college in Greenville, South Carolina, called Furman University. It was my third choice behind the better recognized and more prestigious University of Virginia and University of North Carolina at Chapel Hill. My father received his master's and doctorate at UNC and was a professor at UVA, so I thought I knew both schools well. Furman was a back-up choice. I didn't know much about the school or the academics, but I fell in love with the place—it's one of the most beautiful campuses I've ever visited.

In retrospect, I believe Furman selected me. Although I majored in business, I had the opportunity to be exposed to many other fields of study that sowed the seeds of discovery in me that later manifested themselves in the creation of this book. Furman required every student to take classes in science, religion, history, and Asian/African studies, among other required courses. The classes outside of my major were some of my most memorable. Three of my favorite classes were Asian Studies, Morality and Politics, and Introduction to Philosophy.

The liberal arts theme did not stop with the curriculum. Students were also required to attend various cultural life programs (CLPs) including plays, lectures, and orchestra recitals. At the time, I was much less enthusiastic about the CLPs as they were called because I thought they interfered with my time; however, with the benefit of hindsight, I realize these events forced me out of my narrow scope of interests. CLPs forced me to enlarge my college experience and exposed me to wonderful musicians, philosophers, and issues of the day I would not have otherwise explored. My years at Furman not only prepared me for my chosen field of business; it also opened the door to the greater questions of life.

You don't have to go to an expensive private school to experience the virtues of a liberal arts education. You can take courses of interest to you at the local community college or university. Although many of these courses are available online, it's important you choose a course offering that includes at least some class time. A course that involves the thoughts, questions, and ideas of others adds a richness and depth to the material. As you continue along the path of lifelong learning, you find that life takes on new meaning and enjoyment.

Study of Philosophy

Philosophy was not a subject I planned to take, but I did so as an elective course. I found the subject fascinating and it held my attention in a way that few other courses did. The word "philosophy" is derived from two Greek words: *philo* (love) and *sophia* (wisdom). Philosophy literally means, "the love of wisdom." Although there are many definitions for wisdom, I think the American Heritage Dictionary defines it best as, "Having the ability to discern or judge what is true, right, or lasting." Therefore, the wise person is someone who strives to live in accordance with what is true.

At its core, philosophy is the study of truth. We're all budding philosophers at one stage or another. From the earliest philosophers like Socrates, Plato, and Aristotle to today, we have been on a quest for truth that applies to all people at all times.

Each of us lives according to our own unique philosophy, though most of us are not aware of it. And while most would agree that living in pursuit of truth and wisdom is a good thing, we move through life without closely examining our "truth," that is, what is most important to us as revealed by the choices we make each day.

According to Socrates, the father of western philosophy, "The greatest good of a man is daily to converse about virtue, and all that concerning which you hear me examining myself and others, and that the life which is unexamined is not worth living."

"The life which is unexamined is not worth living." – Socrates

---

The study of philosophy should not be underestimated in its value to us individually and to society as a whole. It's a window into how we live our lives. We're all called to be more self-aware, to examine what is important to us by where we invest our time and energies. Once we become aware of these things, we can then study our lives more objectively. *Am I happy? Do I feel at peace? How do I handle challenges or situations where things do not go as expected?* Those who do not open themselves up to these questions are either arrogant or lost.

As a society, we continue to see an acceleration of material wants and a push for newer, better, and faster. However, cracks in this way of life are recognized now more than ever before. Those dedicated to the truth are beginning to ask the questions more fundamental to life itself. A recent New York Times article, "In a New Generation of College Students, Many Opt for the Life Examined," highlights the popularity of philosophy as a major.

> Once scoffed at as a luxury major, philosophy is being embraced at Rutgers and other universities by a new generation of college students who are drawing modern-day lessons from the age-old discipline as they try to make sense of their world, from the morality of the war in Iraq to the latest political scandal. The economic downturn has done little, if anything, to dampen this

enthusiasm among students, who say that what they learn in class can translate into practical skills and careers.[18]

Perhaps a new generation of philosophers can slow the momentum of materialism in society.

Life Maps

Dedication to the truth is a way of life, a philosophy of life if you will. It's a commitment to look deep within and question our existing thoughts and beliefs or "maps" of how the world works and how we work effectively within the world. According to Dr. Peck, each of us lives using a unique set of maps that have been developed over time based on our family, friends/social network, and our personal experiences. These maps are used, mostly subconsciously, to form our worldview. As a result, it's very important that our maps be an accurate representation of reality.

Unfortunately, to a greater or lesser degree, our maps contain errors or distortions. Therefore, a key component of a life dedicated to the truth is a commitment to be vigilant in recognizing and then modifying our outdated or distorted maps. Those who are the happiest and most at peace tend to have the most accurate maps and are the most open to modifying their maps when change is needed.

There's no better way to describe how we navigate through life than the map metaphor. Think about the last time you used a map that had errors and outdated information. You might reach your destination, but the journey takes longer. The same is true with our life maps. We often have beliefs or rules that obscure us from the more direct path in life. The problem is we usually have no idea our maps are outdated, so we take the same approach over and over again and wonder why we encounter so much difficulty.

[18] Winnie Hu, "In a New Generation of College Students, Many Opt for the Life Examined," New York Times, April 6, 2008.

If we run into the same obstacles repeatedly at work, with friends, or in a relationship with a significant other, we are likely operating with an unreliable map in need of objective evaluation. Rigorous self-examination and a willingness to be personally challenged are the attributes required to move in a new direction.

IMMUTABLE LAW 6
A life of total dedication to the truth also means
a life willing to be personally challenged.[18]

When my challenges at work were at their peak and we still hadn't sold our house, I decided to see a therapist. This was a difficult decision and only came about because I was desperate to make a change. I never saw myself as someone who needed therapy; I just wanted to relieve this huge level of stress I found myself carrying around. I finally realized the stigma of seeing a therapist was the only thing preventing me from going, so I made the commitment to go.

One of the areas we spent a great deal of time discussing was the importance of truth-telling. Initially, I welcomed this topic because I believed this to be an area of personal strength. Despite my confidence, or maybe because of it, my therapist drilled down into our discussion about honesty and said, "Whenever I hear someone say they are extremely dedicated to the truth my radar goes up."

"Why is that?" I asked. "I know I'm making some mistakes in my job and not living as effectively as I should, but I don't have a problem with the truth!"

[19] Peck, pg. 52

"Ultimately, you are here because you want to face the truth, but you are having difficulty doing so. You must be completely open to seeing the truth in how you are behaving and the way that impacts yourself and others."

"What do you mean?" This whole conversation really annoyed me. Why was he questioning my integrity? "I am here precisely because I want to seek the truth and the truth is important to me. I am a truthful person."

"Is that so?" my therapist said. "Then why are you having so much trouble seeing how your choices are affecting your daily work situation? You have created a defense mechanism that is obscuring the truth in this situation. You are not being honest with yourself."

Only after I reflected on the conversation much later did I began to understand what my therapist was referring to. He wasn't so much questioning whether I tell the truth with others; he wanted to know whether I was honest with myself. In other words, was I open to change in how I viewed the world, or was I hanging on to my outdated maps?

The specific issue centered on my inability to confront some key issues at work and at home that were impacting my ability to be at peace. I developed a whole host of reasons why it didn't make sense to confront these issues with my boss. Ultimately, it was my unwillingness to confront these issues that was creating a significant amount of stress.

Many of us think we want the truth; however, upon closer examination, we're more interested in having our personal "Self Truth" validated by others. I say Self Truth because it's really not truth at all but only our clinging to an outmoded system of beliefs. Instead of an honest appraisal of our maps, we're doing just the opposite: protecting our outdated maps. This defense is really just protecting our own egos. Our egos, or Judging Minds, become the biggest impediment to lasting personal growth. Therefore, it's vital that we use the tools described at the end of the chapter on happiness to create the necessary gaps in thinking and judging through the conscious use of meditation. These gaps allow *awareness* into our lives—awareness of self and truth.

Essential Tools

Living a life dedicated to the truth requires awareness and discipline and, according to Dr. Peck, "a life of continuous and never-ending stringent self-examination."[20] There are three tools that may be used to assist us in living a life dedicated to the truth. They are relatively straightforward and easy to understand but require discipline and awareness to be used effectively. By using these tools consistently, we take more control of our lives and become more conscious of the goals we seek.

1. Non-resistance to reality:

The first and most vital tool in living a life dedicated to the truth involves non-resistance to reality. This can be the most difficult to apply because our outdated maps will often obscure reality. In the example above, I was clinging to my map of being a truthful person. I took a great deal of pride in the fact that I told the truth and was a trustworthy individual. Although it was important to me to tell the truth with others, my therapist pointed out that I was not willing to be a truth-teller with myself. This was at the heart of my problem. My lack of self-honesty obscured the challenges I was facing at work.

You have similar defense or "protection" mechanisms present in your life. These "protection" mechanisms are shielding the ego from the truth and must be removed in order to change our maps. These judgments of truth and trustworthiness are all fabrications of the Judging Mind and ego designed to protect and maintain our sense of self. Awareness of these impediments is critical to seeing the problem

---

[20] Ibid, pg. 51

objectively. Only then are we able to recognize the reality of our behavior and how it impacts our results.

Most of us don't even realize we're resisting reality. From our frame of reference (and outdated maps), we're just experiencing bad luck at work or an unreasonable spouse at home. We may have a trusted friend, mentor, or pastor who is able to help us see how we may be resisting reality, but in most cases a trained therapist is the best choice because they have prior experience dealing with similar issues every day.

In my example above, the problem was right under my nose but I refused to see it until confronted by my therapist, and even then it was a battle between my Judging Self and my Natural Self to expose my resistance to reality. You can't really move forward until you find those obstacles or errors present in your maps. Take the emotion out of the situation and commit yourself to uncovering the ways in which you resist reality. Only then will you be able to accept and make change.

2. Acceptance of change:

Once we remove the barriers to viewing our life situation as it is (non-resistance to reality), we put ourselves in a position to make and be more accepting of change. However, most of us are extremely resistant to change. Why is that? There are three primary reasons:

- **Diminishment of the ego:**
Over time, our ego, or Judging Mind, has built its own set of maps and rules for how the world works. Regardless of how effective they may be, the ego must accept its partial diminishment upon the recognition that its maps are not completely accurate. The ego is designed to protect, maintain, and enhance our concept of self. Any diminishment is a sign of failure and no ego wants to be associated with failure. It's important, however, for us to look deep inside and become self-aware of these protection mechanisms.

As we grow older, the ego becomes entrenched and we become less willing to take risks through experiential learning. Experiential learning is the best and most effective way we learn. Unfortunately, society's pressures make it more difficult for us to fail during this natural learning process. Instead, we become more concerned with how we appear to others: *Do I drive the right car? Do I live in the right neighborhood? Am I wearing the right clothes? Am I putting forth the right image to those I meet?* These "concerns of the world," as Jesus put it, obscure our focus from the most important things.

Whatever small diminishment the ego may encounter through change will be more than overcome by living with more accurate maps. It's through the gaps of thought that we may become aware of our behavior and willing to risk diminishment of the ego for our own betterment.

• *Fear of the unknown:*

Change requires that we be comfortable with the unknown. Although we may recognize the need for change, actually taking the steps to change our behavior exposes us to uncertainty. It's important to acknowledge the spiritual element involved in successful change. Spirituality requires that we walk in *faith* knowing that our Creator wants us to realize our dreams and become successful. Walking in faith is required whenever we embark on change; whether it be a career change, marriage, or any other change in which fear of the unknown is present.

Effectively navigating the unknown is best done through a deep, abiding faith, meditation, and prayer. Fears are created by the ego to protect itself from loss. But this protection mechanism often prevents us from becoming our best.

Quieting the ego through meditation is the best way to silence the fears that can stifle our growth and development.

The role of spirituality and faith will be discussed in detail in later chapters. For now, it's important to realize they may be the key enablers of our ability to change. For many, it's the best way to combat all sorts of fears, including fear of the unknown.

• *Pull of materialism:*

In the "Bondage of Debt" chapter, we discussed the world's preoccupation with more and better stuff and our material wants and desires. Although we may find ourselves stuck in a job or lifestyle we no longer find valid or fulfilling, it's difficult to get off of the treadmill of keeping up with the Joneses. Whenever we cling to materialism at the expense of our own inner peace, the truth becomes obscured.

You may be in a situation right now where you feel trapped by a lifestyle of material commitment: the fancy car, the clothes, a house you can't afford. Although it may be difficult to make big, visible changes quickly, you can develop a plan to reduce debt over the next three to five years (remember it is best to come up with a specific goal). Using the tools discussed in Chapter Three, you can develop a plan and set of goals designed to free yourself from the trap of materialism.

Take a step back from your current life situation. How much is your resistance to change based on a fear of job loss or the challenging job market? Once you put yourself in a financial situation in which you have cushion, you will find you're no longer a prisoner to your worries and fears. You may begin to take more risks in your current job because you recognize that you can fail and still be in a position to do something else.

Financial freedom isn't just for the very wealthy; it can be available to each of us based upon a willingness to live within our means. Become responsible for your own saving and spending habits. Resolve to free yourself from fears caused by the treadmill of material wants and desires.

3. Alignment of inner and outer purpose:

I had just purchased (financed) my dream home in Marietta. My father lived close by and many weekends would come over to watch a football or baseball game with the family. I distinctly remember one of these visits when it was just the two of us and during a break in the game I asked him, "Is this all there really is?"

I caught him off-guard. Lost in thought, he looked at me rather quizzically and asked, "What do you mean?"

"You know, the big house is nice and all, but it's not what I expected. I remember the first time I walked in this house and it was pretty awesome; I felt like a king. But now I'm used to it and am no longer as taken with it. I definitely like my home, but it hasn't changed me. I feel like there's something more to life than this."

My poor dad—he had no idea what to say. I can't remember exactly what he did say but it went something like this: "Dave, this house is amazing. I have never even dreamed of living in a place as nice as this." He kept going. "I am so proud of how successful you have been in your career at such a young age. You have so much more life ahead of you and should feel good about how you are living life to this point."

Those who live on the highest plane of effectiveness, peace, and happiness enjoy an alignment of inner and outer purpose that most people can only envy. Most of us ask the questions at some point in our lives: *Why am I here? What is my life's purpose?* In reality, we answer these questions each and every day by how we live. However, attempting to answer them with the same certainty as *How do I boil a pot of water?* is another thing entirely. Eckhart Tolle provides some of the most insightful guidance on the topic of alignment in his writings and teachings. In *A New Earth*, he takes this very difficult and challenging topic and distills it to its essence:

> So the most important thing to realize is this: your life has an inner purpose and an outer purpose. Inner purpose concerns Being and is primary. Outer purpose concerns Doing and is secondary . . . Inner and outer, however, are so intertwined that it is almost impossible to speak of one without referring to the other.
>
> Your inner purpose is to awaken. It is as simple as that. You share that purpose with every other person on the planet—because it is the purpose of humanity. Your inner purpose is an essential part of the purpose of the whole, the universe and its emerging intelligence. Your outer purpose can change over time. It varies greatly from person to person. Finding and living in alignment with the inner purpose is the foundation for fulfilling your outer purpose. It is the basis for true success. Without that alignment, you can still achieve certain things through effort, struggle, determination, and sheer hard work or cunning. But there is no joy in such endeavor, and it invariably ends in some form of suffering.[21]

Awakening or becoming conscious of our connection with all of life is therefore a primary truth. Finding ways in which we can live our lives through our family relationships, vocation, and social connections to express our inner purpose is how the outer purpose becomes manifested. The unique gifts, skills, and personalities that each of us

[21] Eckhart Tolle, A New Earth (London: Penguin Publishing, 2005), pg. 258.

possess provides the best clues for living a life in which our outer purpose may be connected with inner purpose.

Call to Action

In John 8:32 (NIV) Jesus says, "You will know the truth, and the truth will set you free." Are we dedicated to the truth or are we wed to our outdated maps? In order to be set free, we must remove the shackles that bind us to our outdated maps. These shackles are ego, pride, and fear of change. The bravest thing we can do is recognize that our maps are no longer working and begin the process of change.

Truth is not relative.

Truth is not relative. It will not change. Many difficulties in life are a result of living in conflict with the truth; therefore, we must be open to change. If an aspect of our life isn't working and we find ourselves repeating the same mistakes over and over again, it's time to take a look at our maps.

I was not facing the truth about my fear of confrontation and how that was limiting my performance at work and at home. I made one excuse after another, putting the blame on others rather than facing this truth. Why? Because facing this truth about myself was painful. It made me feel as though I were failing. It was much easier to hide this truth than to face the pain and challenge of looking for ways to change. However, once I began to accept this truth and the discipline of changing how I handled conflict, I became more at peace with myself.

Proactively handling conflict does not mean putting other people on the spot or creating friction and disruption for its own sake. Rather, it just means calmly facing a pain point with others and looking for ways to handle that challenge in an open, productive manner. It's one thing to be truthful in business dealings or leveling with your spouse when we've made a mistake, but quite another to look deeply within and honestly evaluate personal truth-telling. Lying to ourselves is the worst possible lie, but the one we're most likely to make. We have created a host of defense mechanisms to protect ourselves from the truth because the truth might bring short-term pain.

Which do you want to choose, short-term pain or long-term misery?

If we find ourselves making the same mistakes over and over again, we must take a fresh look at our maps and be willing to make changes. Dedication to the truth is a very personal issue. It gets at the heart of how effective we are in living. I believe most of us want to be truthful about ourselves and the lives we lead. However, we all are impacted by various experiences that, over time, create a distorted view of how we see the truth. A commitment to personal growth and development is a commitment to truth-telling. Such a commitment will reward us with a renewed confidence in our ability to grow and become better in all that we do.

Key Takeaways:

1. Truth may be defined as conformity with reality, and more broadly as the natural laws of the universe.

2. The ego or Judging Mind often places Self Truth above "Truth." The resulting conflict often manifests itself through incomplete or inaccurate maps of the world.

3. A liberal arts education helps broaden our perspective beyond a single field of study. Consider taking a college or university class in which you might have an interest.

4. Philosophy comes from Greek words that mean "love of wisdom." There is an increase in philosophy majors as students recognize the value in leading a life of wisdom.

5.   A life dedicated to the truth means a willingness to be personally challenged and to make changes.

6. The tools required for living a life dedicated to the truth are:
   a. non-resistance to reality,
   b. acceptance of change,
   c. alignment of inner and outer purpose.

7. Impediments to change are:
   a. diminishment of the ego,
   b. fear of the unknown,
   c. pull of materialism.

8. Our inner purpose is concerned with "being" and its primary goal is to awaken.

9. Our outer purpose is concerned with "doing." It's important to utilize our gifts and guiding principles in formation of our outer purpose.

10. We have a better chance of realizing our inner purpose when our outer purpose is in harmony with our gifts and guiding principles.

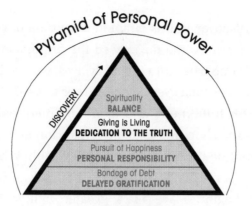

CHAPTER 7

GIVING IS LIVING

"Give, and it will be given to you. A good measure, pressed down,
shaken together and running over, will be poured into your lap."
– Luke 6:38 (NIV)

One of life's great truths involves giving, but most of us are blind to this truth through a life consumed with fear and lack. Competition and scarcity are such a part of our daily routine that giving is often reduced as an afterthought rather than a priority. The thinking goes, If I have something left over after all my needs are met, I'll consider giving. However, this thinking completely misses the point and power of giving.

Over time, the more we give, the more we get in return. Giving not only involves our material wealth, but also the giving of ourselves to family, friends, and neighbors in need. Giving could be called "love in action."

Giving is love in action.

As we will discover in this chapter, extending ourselves through giving brings blessings that far exceed the original act. If we would incorporate this one truth into our daily lives, we would realize more peace and happiness than ever before. Why is this so? Ultimately, we're all on a quest for fulfillment, and true fulfillment only comes from living a life of expansion and growth. Expansion and growth require effort and cannot be bought with material wealth. When we take the leap of faith into a life filled with giving of ourselves, our wealth, and our time, we begin to see life's greater truths. Love becomes manifested through our willingness to give.

IMMUTABLE LAW 7
Giving requires discipline.

The Discipline of Giving

Giving is a discipline. This is a great truth that must be completely understood to appreciate the challenge of giving. It's said that some people are naturally "givers" and some are naturally "takers," but this description is a gross over-simplification. Most of us fall somewhere between givers and takers depending on our stage in life, a given situation, and personality type.

Giving isn't a natural act. Our entire genetic make-up has been developed over the centuries to protect and guard our selves first. We're all born "me oriented." Survival of the fittest and fight-or-flight reflexes are programmed into us—hard-wired you might say—to protect and preserve our well-being. These protection devices have served us quite well; so why should we strive to develop a giving mindset?

The act of giving isn't always easy, but it gets easier with practice. The more we give of ourselves, the more we receive in return. Think of giving as planting seeds in a garden. Any gardener knows that sowing seeds properly will yield exponentially more seeds in the form of the fruit and grain of mature plants. Just as this law of nature means that we reap more seeds than we sow, so it goes with giving.

> *The more we give of our selves, time, and money,*
> *the more we receive in return.*

Words of caution about giving are needed at the outset. I consider these the "fool's gold" of giving in that they may appear to be genuine giving at first, but upon further examination are not acts of true giving at all.

First, giving is not about scorekeeping or transactions:

When we do a favor for someone and expect it to be returned at a later date, we aren't truly giving. Instead, we're striking a bargain: I will watch your kids after school tomorrow, but I need you to pick up my kids from baseball practice on Wednesday.

> *Giving is not about scorekeeping or transactions.*

To borrow a term from economics, I call this a bargain transaction, because our giving is done in exchange for a future favor. There is nothing implicitly wrong with this behavior, but it's not true giving. A bargain is a transaction in which we receive a value approximately equal to what we invested. If that individual does not repay us in a manner expected, then we'll no longer participate in that transaction. It's quite common to confuse giving with bargain transactions. We often feel frustrated that our "giving gestures" are not repaid; however, such feelings are a sure sign the initial act was not true giving.

Second, don't expect a "giving ATM" to show up in your home:

As we become more giving people we might think: Wow, I've really been giving a lot lately. I must have substantial giving "deposits" in the bank. *Time to make a withdrawal from my giving ATM!* We have no control over these "withdrawals." Giving comes back to us over time, in surprising and often imperceptible ways. There's no immediate gratification in giving except in the act itself. True giving, by its nature, is not transactional. Giving is done out of unselfish love for the benefit of someone else. I have found, however, that the more giving I become the more I receive. This increase is almost imperceptible at first, but over time, our seeds of giving will begin to multiply with abundant fruit.

Third, giving is not about being a doormat:

A "doormat" is someone who is routinely taken advantage of, but who hides behind a false sense of being a giver. A true giver is someone who is in control of the giving. It's done out of free will, not out of obligation or a poor self-image. In fact, giving in a "doormat" manner isn't giving at all, but is simply being taken advantage of. When we feel we're being used, it hurts us and often builds resentment in our approach to life.

Giving is an effort-filled activity. If we happen to be extremely well-off financially, we are capable of giving a lot. But if our giving takes the form of a tax write-off managed by our accountant and not us, it's tax planning, not giving. Jesus emphasizes this point in Luke 12:48 (NIV) when he says, "From everyone who has been given much, much will be demanded; and from the one who has been entrusted with much, much more will be asked." When we're financially well-off, it's important to maintain a sense of grace and gratitude rather than entitlement. We must seek ways to pay our good fortune forward through church and community activities.

From everyone who has been given much, much will be demanded; and from the one who has been entrusted with much, much more will be asked."
– Luke 12:48 (NIV)

As a corporate and investment banker, I've spent considerable time with CEOs and CFOs of public and private companies who have accumulated a great deal of wealth. At their best, I've found these people are bright, hard working, and humble about their achievements. But at their worst, I've encountered many who have a chip on their shoulder and think they are gifted above all others. This arrogance is so misplaced! Yes, they worked hard and were smart, but their success is a gift from God that should humble them.

How many times have we seen the fall of the giant egos? Whether it's a fall in their personal lives due to their singular focus on work without the balance of family, or the switching from one job to another in the belief that their magical skills and abilities are transferable to any situation, the hubris and arrogance some people develop through material success is often a poison that kills their joy for the wonders of life. No matter how successful we are, it's vital to stay humble in our achievements and see them as an opportunity to do more for others. We should bask in life's blessings rather than our own arrogance.

In summary, giving is a discipline that must be practiced in order to be mastered. It's not a natural act for most people, and we should not expect giving to be easy. However, the fruits of giving can transform our lives. These fruits do not become manifested in an "I do this for you, and you do this for me" equation or bargain transaction, but over time, we begin to reap the benefits. The act of giving out of our own free will produces a sense of peace and improves our self-image. Giving is a renewing, spiritual act that brings us closer to our fellow human beings and deepens our spiritual lives, bringing us closer to the truth—to God.

The Giving Habit

Because it's difficult for many people to give (including myself), it's necessary to begin by creating a giving habit. The secret to any life change is to create new good habits. Each one of us is a creature of habits—some good and some bad. The key to self-improvement is to crowd out our bad habits by starting better ones. I found giving to be an area where I needed to develop a more healthy habit. I did not feel I was giving appropriately in many areas of my life including church, so I decided to start there.

At that time I wasn't in the habit of going to church. I averaged once a month attendance and had a host of very good excuses such as being too tired, difficulty getting kids ready, and so on. Meanwhile, Kim and I were sending our children to the parish school of religion for first communion preparation. How could we send them to this program every Tuesday and yet miss most Sundays at church? What message were we sending our kids?

Giving at Church

Once Kim and I developed the habit of going *to* church, it became rather obvious that we needed to develop the habit of giving *at* church. The first way we began to give at church was in the offertory. We did not pledge a certain level of giving; we just began to give modestly in the weekly collection. Since our initial level of giving was small, it had no impact on our lifestyle; it just became another habit.

Next, we participated in adopting a family at Christmas—a single mother with three boys— and we committed to buying, wrapping, and delivering gifts for them. This was a bigger commitment than we had initially expected both financially and logistically. We were very busy with our own plans and obligations. However, Kim said the feeling of satisfaction she felt when she went down to the church to deliver the presents was truly life-affirming. The church was full of Christmas gifts for hundreds of families. There were trucks filled with presents. It was as though Santa had a satellite workshop and his helpers were there in force. Kim involved our kids in shopping and finding gifts on this family's list. It became a family project on giving and expanded our appreciation of the true meaning of Christmas.

Finally, the big test arrived. The church needed a new, larger sanctuary to accommodate its growing membership. A capital campaign commenced and pledges were solicited over a three-year period. This was a level of giving we would not have been prepared to participate in if we had not begun the habits of giving described above. By developing these giving habits at church, we had a much better perspective of how we were impacting the community.

We've only just begun. I'm not even close to where I want to be in my level of giving at church, but the point is, I would not be where I am now if it wasn't for these small habits that grew in to bigger habits of giving. I'm still exercising my giving muscles, and I realize deep down inside that I'm not giving as much as I can or should. My giving at church continues to be a work in progress and I have a long way to go. We continue to struggle with ways the family can become more involved in the church community through volunteer activities. The important thing for me is to be on the giving path. I know we can and we will do better as I grow in faith and lessen my grasp on the material world.

Giving at Work

Do you ever feel like you're bombarded with giving requests at work? It starts with our employers strongly encouraging us to give to the United Way through the yearly campaign. Next, we have fund raisers throughout the year for worthy causes such as the March of Dimes, the American Heart Association, Susan G. Komen for the Cure, and American Cancer Society. I remember a feeling of impatience and resentment regarding these fund-raising campaigns. Why? I felt I'd given enough when I made my commitment to the United Way and our commitments to church.

Now I see these giving opportunities in a different light. All are worthy causes and I challenge you to give to these fund-raisers enthusiastically! Put yourself in the position of your colleagues who are leading the effort. They are volunteering their time; it's hard work; it's awkward to ask for donations. Make it easy on them and on yourself by making a habit of giving to these worthy causes. Pick a number that works for you—$10, $20, or $5—and do it! You'll be a hero to your fellow employees and it will make you feel better about yourself. You're giving more than to the individual charity; you're giving of yourself to your colleagues and they will be grateful. Once you decide up front to give to these fund-raisers, it makes the actual giving more enjoyable.

Don't stop with these worthy fund-raisers. You can support your friend's daughter as she raises money (and self-confidence) through Girl Scout cookie sales, or by purchasing raffle tickets for a school project. Also, consider being a part of the next Habit for Humanity project your company sponsors. Giving in these areas at work will bring you closer to your associates and create common bonds. I don't care whether you like Girl Scout cookies; give them away if you want. The point is to develop a habit of giving at work and to do so cheerfully. It will make you feel good and will enhance your reputation as a team player.

Giving in the Community

Churches and schools create bonds that cement communities together. I believe the community has lost some of its bonding due to an erosion of the community school. Many options exist that result in families from the same community sending their children to multiple schools. As a result, community giving takes more effort in today's world of private schools—not to mention the Internet's virtual community—and the multiple demands of our time. That being said, community isn't less important today than it was years ago.

Before Kim and I had children, I became involved in a community organization called "Hands on Nashville." One of Hands on Nashville's community efforts was a parks revitalization project. I remember leading the volunteer efforts at work to clean up an inner-city park that had fallen into neglect and disrepair. The park needed trash collection, weeds pulled, and mulch spread in order to become usable as a playground. It was a big job and I found it very difficult to get my colleagues to volunteer. My boss, Walker Choppin, saw I was having trouble and committed to working on Saturday. What a difference his leadership made in staffing the project!

I was able to get enough people to help and we turned that neglected playground into a beautiful new park that the community could take pride in. I will never forget the effort that Walker put into the project. He was the first one to get to the site, the last one to leave, and the one who worked the hardest. His example really made an impact on me; it emphasized how he invested in all areas of life, not just at work.

Commit yourself to the community and watch the bonds of friendship that develop!

One of the biggest barriers toward cheerful and willing giving is our own internal perspective on life. Is the cup half full or half empty? Do we see the world as an abundant place full of unlimited opportunity or a battleground where we must protect what is ours? Ultimately, the answers to these questions reveal our willingness to give.

Abundance vs. Scarcity Mentality:

To create a giving mindset, we need to understand the thinking that makes it so difficult for us to give. At its core, we don't give because we don't think we have enough to give. Whether that stems from a poor self-image that assumes what we have to give doesn't matter, or from a belief that we can't afford to give, both mindsets represent a scarcity mentality. A scarcity mentality is an easy habit to develop. We're taught from an early age to save our pennies and not be wasteful. These are good habits; however, it's rarely overspending on others that results in trouble. Instead, we get into trouble with our spending when we're completely focused on ourselves.

Money is but one of many areas where we become "lack-minded." We're lack-minded when we don't give time to our children, our spouse, and our church, or when feelings of envy or bitterness crop up when a friend or family member experiences success. Becoming lack-minded is the worst thing we can do to ourselves as it creates more lack and sucks us into a negative downward spiral:

DOWNWARD SPIRAL

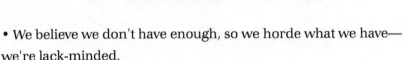

• We become even more grasping—
this results in failure, unhappiness
and poor self-image.

• "Lack-minded" and
"Competition" cycles begin
again from an even lower
place—we become even
more closed and our ability to give is further stunted.

• We believe we don't have enough, so we horde what we have—
we're lack-minded.

• Someone else's victory becomes our failure—competition for
finite resources.

Eric Kimani gave a speech to the Kenya Institute of Bankers on December 1, 2006 that articulated the differences between the Scarcity and Abundance mentalities and showed how they impacted growth and development in his home in Kenya. Eric and his wife, Margaret, are entrepreneurs who started with a few dairy cows in 1987 and grew a very humble dairy business into Palmhouse Dairies Limited, which produces more than 3,000 liters of milk per day and supplies the most respected institutions in Nairobi.

Eric knows what scarcity is all about; he has been surrounded by it his entire life, yet he never felt as though his life would be about scarcity. He is not only an entrepreneur, but also a motivational change agent in his country and beyond. Listen to what he has to say about the scarcity mentality:

> The scarcity mentality is a belief that our success will imply someone else's failure; that there are scarce resources and if we get them we must deny someone else; that there is scarcity of jobs; that the cake is not enough and I must grab my share. The scarcity mentality is one of our biggest problems in this country today with politicians believing that they have gone to parliament to ensure they get the largest share of the national cake for their people/electorate.
>
> This was also epitomized lately by a senior executive friend of mine whom I approached in September to donate money to the national charitable cause I referred to above that incidentally helps more people from his village than anywhere else in Kenya. He responded that he could not help because they have a similar initiative to help his village. His scarcity mentality—that there is not enough for his village and the national initiative blinded him in seeing that he could

achieve what he is doing for the village in a more far-reaching manner.[22]

Eric contrasts the scarcity mentality with traits that are seen in the abundance mentality:

> People with an abundance mentality have an internal security based on principle-centered living. Their value system is self-anchored. They are not too worried of saying/doing the wrong thing because they ordinarily talk from a point of truth. This frees their mind to bigger/better thoughts because they have nothing to cover. What they said yesterday is what they will repeat today without contradiction. This internal security enhances their

UPWARD SPIRAL

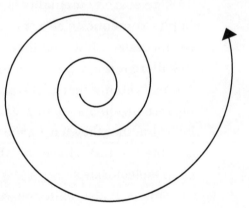

• Guiding principles provide
an anchor of self-belief
and respect.

• Self-confidence allows us
to be more generous with
ourselves and our resources.

• As we give, we enjoy
more satisfaction and peace in our lives.

• Our giving results in blessings multiplied and in more fulfilled lives.

---

[22] Eric Kimani, "The Abundance versus Scarcity Mentality in Professional Development and Growth", Nairobiliving.com, December 1, 2006.

humility. It allows them to enjoy professional freedom. They can choose what they want to do. By contrast, people with a scarcity mentality seek their validation from groups. They will rarely want to take action on their own. The group must validate what they do.[23]

Eric's description of an abundance mentality includes concepts like "principle-centered," "point of truth," and "professional freedom" that are all expressed in this book. By choosing an abundance mentality, we choose a path that pulls us upward in a positive living-and-giving cycle.

Creation vs. Competition:

Consider how an abundance mentality impacts our view of the world. Instead of competing for finite resources, attention, or our "share," we're thinking creatively. How can I do things differently? How can I capitalize on my unique strengths and gifts?

Think about some of the most successful companies formed over the years such as Starbucks, Apple, and Harley-Davidson. These companies operate in highly competitive markets, yet their growth trajectories and operating margins are far more impressive than other companies in these same sectors. Why? I think it's because they have created something totally unique. They are not really competing in the traditional sense; instead, they are creating a unique experience.

Why not commit yourself to the same level of uniqueness? Instead of emulating your neighbors or your friends, embrace your own gifts and be the best that you are meant to be.

Giving in Marriage

Perhaps the most important yet overlooked area in which we should give is in our marriages. A strong marriage is the foundation in

---

[23] Ibid.

all we do, but how many of us take the relationship with our spouses for granted? This is natural because our spouses and families are so familiar; however, I encourage you to not overlook this relationship.

My relationship with Kim has evolved over the years. We had one type of relationship before having children and a different kind now that we have two kids. As the children grow, our relationship grows, changes, and adapts. I've found that our effectiveness as parents, at work, and in the community can be traced back to how effective or "in tune" we are with each other. All marriages and relationships are different, but there are some key things that consistently make them stronger.

Start Here First:

By "Start Here First," I mean we must make the marriage relationship a priority. Since this is the most important relationship we have on earth, it's vital that we continually give of ourselves to our spouses. It's this giving and investing that is true love in action. It takes discipline and effort to put marriage first in our lives because it is so familiar to us. I find it important to incorporate "marriage-first" items into my daily planner or I'm unsuccessful in keeping this special commitment.

Guys, how hard is it to stop by the grocery store on the way home and buy your wife flowers and/or a bottle of wine? How about arranging for a babysitter so you can enjoy dinner and a movie? When I incorporate these simple tasks into my daily routine, it's not hard to get these special nights planned. However, when I don't plan these things and write them down, I seldom make the events happen. Why? I don't hold myself accountable when the idea is just in my head. For me, writing it on paper as a "to-do" item memorializes the idea and creates a sense of urgency in getting it accomplished. These are small things, but small things add up to big things. You must do the little things over the course of time to keep the relationship fresh.

Ladies, what should you add to your list?

Start Here First is the most important rule to achieving and maintaining a strong marriage, but all of our other commitments will conspire to break this rule. We're overcommitted at work and at home with school events and kids' athletics. It's vital to be faithful to our first commitment (marriage) before we become overcommitted in these other areas.

There's a very personal dimension for me in the idea of Start Here First. My mom and dad were wonderful parents who encouraged, developed, and supported my sisters and me as we grew up. The family unit was especially important for us due to the many moves we made as a result of my father's job and career changes. If not for this strong family unit, I would have struggled mightily as the "new kid" in all the different towns.

My parents had been married for forty years. Despite their long-term relationship and success in raising a good family, my parents recently finalized their divorce. Their divorce has been a personal wake-up call for me in my own marriage. It has resulted in soul searching and asking *Why?* and *What can I do differently?* Even though I will never understand the intricacies of their relationship and won't be able to completely know what happened, I've gained insight based on my own relationship with Kim.

Over time, through my dad's focus on career and my mom's focus on family, they invested less and less time in their marriage. They struggled, as we all do, with Start Here First. When we kids had grown and moved on with our own lives, Mom and Dad were left with each other. They discovered they had grown apart and did not have enough other common interests to make the marriage work.

This has been extremely difficult for me, but it has renewed my commitment not to let the same thing happen. I can see the commitments and separate lives that Kim and I live conspiring to put our marriage in second place. It's as subtle as sand eroding away at high tide and nearly as imperceptible. Don't let it happen! Remember to invest time and energy in your marriage first in order to nourish your most important relationship.

Communicate what's important:

Silence is deadly in a relationship. So too is fighting and bickering over everyday challenges. Communication is part art and part science and demands patience! Picking a fight over small things is never a good idea, but ignoring important needs over long periods may be equally damaging to the relationship. The key is in the communication.

The what, when, and how of communication determine how effective we'll be in conveying our needs and feelings. If we only communicate needs when we're frustrated, angry, or upset, we won't be able to achieve the desired outcome in communication. Instead, we'll find our spouses reacting defensively, leading to arguments and misunderstandings. Instead of conveying needs with the goal of changing behavior and living a more harmonious life, we'll be building walls and perpetuating negative cycles. When this doomed mode of communication meets its ultimate failure, we may decide it isn't worth disturbing the peace; rather, we reach a form of understanding more akin to the détente between the Soviet Union and the United States during the Cold War.

Actually, communication is the wrong word for this type of cycle. I consider this to be "venting." By venting, I mean long periods of surface peace and tranquility and then, during a period of moderate stress over minor issues, the venting of our true needs, desires, or frustrations in an emotional way. Venting will happen

[24] Covey, pg. 71.

in any relationship, and there's nothing wrong with occasional venting when tensions are high or we're under stress. The goal, however, is to keep venting to an absolute minimum, and to focus instead on a real dialogue with our spouses.

At the foundation of Stephen Covey's *The Seven Habits of Highly Effective People* is the concept of proactivity. According to Dr. Covey, proactivity "means more than merely taking initiative. It means that as human beings, we are responsible for our own lives. We can subordinate feelings to values. We have the initiative and the responsibility to make things happen."[24] Think for a moment how powerful we could be by subordinating feelings for values. Dr. Covey goes on to say that all receive multiple stimuli from our environment, and we're ultimately responsible for our responses to these stimuli.

Proactivity or "freedom to choose" allows us to determine how we respond to each stimulus, including, of course, the stimulus from a spouse. We can either react defensively when our spouses confront us with a problem in the relationship or we can honor that communication by proactively changing the way our behavior negatively impacts our relationships. The choice is ours. We either continue a cycle of venting followed by a strained effort to keep the peace or we move forward with proactive dialogue that looks for ways to improve the relationship.

In the short term, a venting cycle of communication may be able to keep the marriage together for the sake of the kids, but it will likely not be as successful once the kids are grown and out of the house. Making the silent trade-off of "I won't bring up this issue of mine unless you bring up that issue of yours" is no way to grow a relationship. In most cases, Kim and I did a good job communicating our feelings in a constructive way—except when that communication involved money.

Money is an area in which Kim and I have struggled to reach common ground on several occasions. Like most couples, money has been an area of friction between us to a lesser or greater extent over the years. Since money was a sensitive issue, we tried our best to avoid the topic. Don't get me wrong; we spent time at the beginning of each year developing a budget and dividing up responsibility for various bills, but inevitably our efforts were derailed when unplanned expenses came up. We're both bankers by training and vocation. Managing money should be an area of strength for us; however, it became an area where venting was common. It became especially acute after Kim decided to stay at home after the birth of our second child rather than return to the workplace.

Kim rightfully felt that I was grilling her on a monthly basis regarding her expenses. From my perspective, I couldn't understand why we were not able to stay on budget. From her perspective, she couldn't be expected to know ahead of time all the expenses involved in raising two young children. Our monthly venting sessions usually occurred just after the credit card bill arrived and I did my best detective impersonation seeking answers to our failing budget.

Of course, this line of questioning and venting did not go over well with Kim. She was a little defensive and perhaps fearful of our financial situation. She knew it was important for our spending to be kept in check and for budgets to be hit, but she was a new mother and foreseeing the twists and turns of family spending was a challenge for both of us.

I'd like to say I utilized Dr. Covey's proactivity principle right away, but it took much longer for me to show any further proactivity beyond the annual budget for almost five years. After a particularly painful venting session, We finally came up with a better way. Kim did not have full control of her financial situation and she needed control, not just over a month but for a whole year so she could account for life's little surprises.

The specifics of our solution aren't the main point. What works for us might not work for you. Instead, the point is that it was a proactive solution (finally!) that eliminated a venting cycle in our relationship. The venting over bills was hurting our relationship and proved to be a lousy way to deal with the very real problem of money management. If we had continued along this path of communication, our money problems would have caused severe relationship problems.

Growth and improvement in any area of life is a result of focus and effort. Marriage is no different. As a result, we must communicate when we experience difficulty in the relationship. The goal is to foster an environment of open communication to solve minor problems before they become major. However, if the problems and the breaks in communication become too severe, then seek out a therapist to help facilitate the dialogue. A therapist has the ability to see issues from an objective vantage point. We're often too close to the situation to accurately assess our own limitations and behavioral blind spots.

A therapist will also be able to limit the emotional voltage of the conversation and help focus on the underlying issues that may be getting in the way of open communication. To meet our joint needs for a healthy, fulfilling relationship, we must communicate and then work to fulfill our needs. The more effort we give to our spouses through improved communication, the more we will find the relationship giving back to us.

Develop a common interest:

Kim is an excellent cook and has a real passion for taking everyday dishes and changing the ingredients to make them incredibly unique. Aren't I lucky! I've been on the receiving end of her creative menus for the last fifteen years and I've encouraged her to do her own cookbook. It was not until recently that I found a way to share in her interest for cooking beyond eating her creations. I did, however, and it's made her passion an interest for me that I never thought I would have. Kim will tell you that it's even more fun for her to create menus now that I'm creating some dishes of my own. Here's what happened.

I started to watch the Food Network.

I did not do this of my own free will; I think there was some divine intervention here! Yes, guys, I'm secure enough in my manhood to admit that I watch cooking shows. But, I assure you, it was completely by accident. I began watching the Food Network while using the gym at work. The gym was pretty modest but it did have two TVs along with the requisite workout equipment. It was never crowded because there was a fancy workout facility across the street, but there were a few brave souls who used the facility because we liked the price—free!

Whoever made it first to the gym during lunch determined what the rest of us would watch. It was usually a race between me and two others who frequented the gym. If I won we watched CNBC; if they won it was Food Network. Finally, I gave up racing and watched a couple episodes of Ina Garten's *Barefoot Contessa*. Before I knew it, I was hooked. Her cooking style was very similar to Kim's and I told Kim I liked the show.

Soon, we were recording *Barefoot Contessa* episodes and watching them together after the kids went to bed. I then took a very risky step of pulling together some of my favorite recipes to make dinner for the whole family. With help from Kim, I was able to pull it off! Cooking has turned into a very fun thing Kim and I do together. There have been a few missteps along the way such as cutting off my fingertip when attempting to dice vegetables, and burning my hand after forgetting to use a potholder on a hot skillet, but all in all, this has been fun for both of us.

I've expanded my horizons and cooked for the family while giving Kim a break. My interest has even furthered Kim's passion for creating unique recipes and delicious dishes. We enjoy going to the local Trader Joe's or Whole Foods to select fresh ingredients. We like talking about ways we could cook for a group using ideas from the Food Network and the *Barefoot Contessa*. I'm still waiting for Kim to develop an interest in all things automotive, but that has yet to happen.

My sister and her husband are riding and running together and recently did a team triathlon with my uncle. My sister swam, my brother-in-law biked, and my uncle ran. What is your common interest with your spouse? If nothing now, what could it be? Involvement in kids' activities doesn't count. This is about discovering common interests that will last after the kids are grown and out of the house. This is about investing in the most important relationship we have outside of our relationship with God.

Explore common interests and discover how fulfilling your relationship can be.

Giving to our Children

Our children have a way of reflecting back to us how we are doing as parents. Giving our time, love, and instruction is so important to their development. They are sponges who observe all we do and say and then emulate our words and actions so well it's as though we're looking into a mirror. In most cases this is a good thing, but sometimes they have a way of pointing out our flaws or anxieties.

Do we see stress, fear, and anxiety in our children? If so, it's a good bet they are taking these cues from us. Are our children picky eaters, or easily discouraged? Once again, we need to look at our own behavior, and our own approaches to the difficulties in life. Thank goodness for the forgiving hearts of our children! If it wasn't for my children's resilience, I would not be nearly the father I am today. They teach me as much about myself as I learn about them.

Time and patience:

As new parents, our learning is exclusively on the job, and I, for one, frequently make mistakes. As much as I'd like to believe I "have it down" or that I've "figured them out," my children enter new stages and encounter new challenges that require me to grow and learn as a parent.

A recurring theme throughout these new stages is the need for patience. When we give our children patience, we're giving one of the most important things we have—our time. We're telling them, no matter what the underlying issue, "You are important to me; you have my undivided attention." Giving my time, even when I don't have enough for myself, is always rewarded in the long run.

Sports activities demand a significant time investment from Kim and me—especially the head coaching of Jack's baseball team. It's often a struggle to coordinate practice schedules and games, but we've found the effort very rewarding. We've become a closer family through our common interest in sports and the lessons they teach. Maybe of equal importance, our sports commitments keep us away from the television and stimulate our minds in a real-world activity.

Not every child or adult is interested in sports. There are hundreds of activities, clubs, and associations that can provide quality life education for you and your children, such as:

Activities:	Organizations:
Camping	Boy Scouts
Astronomy/Star Gazing	Girl Scouts
Hunting/Fishing	Community Sports
Collecting	
Gardening	
Farming	

Positive role model:

One of the best things we can give our children is being at our best as a positive role model. My children inspire me to travel upward on the Pyramid of Personal Power in pursuit of the goal to be my best as a father. This has led to several behavioral changes over the years. My impatience and short temper were some of the most difficult hurdles I had to overcome.

Before I had children I remember commenting to someone who was a mother that I felt prepared for the patience required of being a parent because I'd recently taken up golf. Surely, if I had learned to be patient on the golf course, I would be a patient and loving father. I remember her response was to laugh. Golf can't prepare you for becoming a parent!

She was right. I found that my nerves were often frayed and my fuse was very short as a new father. My fuse was short mostly because of two things: 1) I was insecure as a parent and my insecurities led to stress; 2) I was frustrated at what an incredible time commitment having children proved to be. I never felt as though we (I) could get away from the responsibilities of parenthood. Bye-bye golf game; hello stinky diapers.

I wasn't happy and neither was Kim as my frustrations and bad temper were often directed toward her and only increased our stress as new parents. I didn't like myself when I lost my temper. My loud voice terrified our kids. It was a big adjustment for Kim to live with my short fuse and lack of patience. I knew I needed to change for the good of our relationship and my relationship with the kids.

I began to search for ways I might build patience and be more in control of my emotions. I read books on meditation and began reading the Bible. I worked on applying Dr. Covey's principle of stimulus and response as discussed above. I came to realize that how I felt on the inside was being manifest on the outside. In other words, if I felt good about myself, I tended to be more patient and loving in my relationships. As Matthew 15:18 (AMP) says, "Whatever comes out of the mouth comes from the heart."

"Whatever comes out of the mouth comes from the heart."
– Matthew 15:18 (AMP)

I found that reading the Bible helped me find more grace and compassion for others. Giving at the church also reinforced those feelings. In addition, spending time in meditation calmed my mind and created more distance between stimulus and response for me. My nerves were not so raw and I was more peaceful and loving inside. These habits resulted in a big change. Over the span of months I became much more calm, patient, and understanding. My roars were kept at a minimum.

No integrity shortcuts:

Do we keep our commitments to our kids? Do we find that we sometimes let our family commitments slip behind work or volunteer commitments? Character is built on a foundation of integrity, and integrity is the habit of doing what we say we're going to do over and over again. The single best habit we can form is to lead by example with our children. Yes, in the short run, we may be able to rely on our position of power as a parent to force them to behave in a certain way; however, that's a house built on sand. It might be expedient to order our children around like little soldiers, but if they see us not fulfilling our commitments—or saying one thing and doing something different—watch out! We will lose their followership. We might be their parents, but in time, we will no longer be their trusted leaders.

Keeping commitments and doing what we say is often extremely difficult, but it's the sum total of these family interactions that will determine whether our kids follow paths of character built on integrity or paths of the "quick fix" or the "fast buck." One example that sticks out for me was playing on my high school tennis team. Dad was my tennis coach growing up and, over time, I developed an infinity for tennis. I made the high school tennis team in the ninth grade and played for three years. (I stopped playing my senior year to focus on more important things such as cars and girls).

I was fortunate to play on a very good team. Two of my years we won the state tournament. During my sophomore season, our team made the state finals, but only the top six players were eligible to compete. I really wanted to go but I was on the bubble—number six on a ten-person team. The team seeding was determined through a ladder system. You had to challenge teammates ahead of you to matches and win in order to move up. There was one guy below me who wanted to play me. I told my dad the situation and he suggested I just delay playing the guy. The state team would be determined at the end of next week, and he thought I should make excuses not to play in order to make the state team.

I didn't feel good about doing it, but I decided to follow my dad's advice. Guess what? My delay tactics didn't work. The tennis coach found out I was never available to play Steve. She was extremely upset and she forced me to play the match the very day she found out about my stalling.

I was miserable because Steve was a friend of mine and I felt bad about my lame excuses. When we met on the court after school, I apologized. He was nervous, too. He felt bad about telling the coach and getting me in trouble. Neither of us played particularly well; we both just wanted to get it over with. I won the match. Unfortunately, the events leading up to the tournament made it unenjoyable. I didn't play well and lost in the first round.

As I look back on it, this was a huge learning experience. I learned that doing the right thing was very important in making my involvement on the team feel right. If I had never played Steve, I would never have felt as though I belonged on that team. Also, I found that taking the easy way out was not easy in the end. The older I get, the more I realize that the easy way out seldom ever is. Doing things the right way is the only way to build character and confidence.

Key Takeaways:

1. Giving is a discipline; it does not come naturally or easily.

2. Giving is not:
    a. A bargain transaction—if I do this for you, you do this for me.
    b. Being a doormat and allowing others to take advantage of us. Giving is done of our own free will.
    c. A tax deduction.

3. The best way to begin giving is to develop a giving habit in all areas of life: church, work, school, and community. Give happily as a habit!

4. The main barrier to joyful giving is the scarcity mentality. Strive to develop an abundance mentality toward life—there's plenty for everyone. Another person's success does not mean my failure.

5. Give to the marriage first; it's the most important relationship.

6. Communication is the key. Make sure we communicate with our spouses the right way. Striving to keep the peace alone will not allow the relationship to grow.

7. Develop common interests to keep the relationship energized and fresh.

8. Family activities, sports, and associations are great ways to give to our children.

9. Our children are sponges who look to us as the leaders of the family; therefore, we must be good role models.

10. We must show our children strong leadership of character and integrity to help them make right choices in their lives.

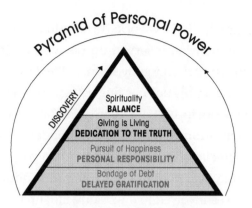

CHAPTER 8

BALANCE

"Be aware of wonder. Live a balanced life—
learn some and think some and draw and paint
and sing and dance and play and work every day some."
–Robert Fulghum

Many remember the movie *City Slickers*, starring Billy Crystal as a burned-out advertising executive in New York looking for a memorable vacation far from the city. He was searching for personal and professional change and thought a vacation with his friends on a working ranch in Colorado would give him the answers needed to get his life back in order. His friends reluctantly agreed to the vacation and off they went on a truly extraordinary adventure. The head cowhand was the crusty and intimidating "Curly" played by the character actor Jack Palance.

Although Mitch, the Billy Crystal character, was scared of Curly (we learn later in the movie that he had killed a man), he recognized the cowboy had some Zen-like wisdom that would help him once he returned to his crazy life in New York. He couldn't help to be drawn to Curly. The wise, old cowhand served up his wisdom in short, funny remarks and then tempted Mitch by saying, "The key to life is just one thing," while holding up his pointer finger to emphasize the point.

The movie came out in 1991, the year I graduated from college, and I thought it was very funny. I didn't fully understand the subtleties of what Mitch was going through with his out-of-control job and life. Now that I've spent twenty years building a career and enduring the twists, turns, and challenges involved in a working life, I have a much better perspective of his yearning for that "one thing."

So, what is that "one thing?" In the movie, Curly whispered to Mitch as he was dying the secret to life. That one thing is—*Balance.*

Billy Crystal's character knew he was living out of balance, being totally consumed by work. Something deep down inside told him to search for what's important, and he was able to do so only after he left his stressful work environment. He had so many blessings around him at home and with his friends, but they were obscured by the stresses of everyday working life!

Many of us live with a vague sense that we're out of balance, but we find it difficult to change. We become consumed by our jobs, calendars, and commitments while the most important things such as marriage, children, friends, and spirituality completely vanish. We find ourselves over-committed and not enjoying the most important things life has to offer. Therefore, it's no mistake that balance is at the top of the pyramid. It's there because we need the other skills discussed in this book (delayed gratification, assumption of responsibility, and dedication to the truth) to attain a life of balance. When we are living in balance, we are at the highest level of living; we are at peace. Balance is the key to a successful, meaningful life.

IMMUTABLE LAW 8
Balance is the key to a successful, meaningful life.

Three Dimensions of Balance

The three dimensions in which we may experience balance are: work/life (W/L), physical/mental (P/M), and material/spiritual (M/S). The first two, W/L and P/M, are aspects of balance we experience in the material world; therefore, I refer to them as balance of the first order. M/S is the balance between the material and spiritual worlds, and I consider it to be balance of the second order.

The summit of the pyramid is achieved when we realize perfect M/S balance. Since it's balance of the second order, it's very difficult to glimpse—let alone to achieve—without first achieving balance in the W/L and P/M realms. The capstone of the pyramid is itself a pyramid and represents the three dimensions of balance: the first two are at the bottom corners of the capstone and the top represents M/S balance. Perfect M/S balance is the ultimate goal, but most of us will only have a fleeting experience here. Does that mean we should not aspire to perfect balance? No. Even brief experiences of M/S balance expand our sense of peace and connectedness with those around us.

I've found that balance in each of these areas requires a great deal of attention, focus, and effort. *Awareness* allows us to objectively view how balanced we are in each of these dimensions. Our willingness to *tell the truth* will determine how successful we are in attaining both first and second order balance. As we navigate the issues of life, it's vital we strive for balance in the W/L and P/M areas. First order balance creates stability and maximizes our effectiveness. Let's look at both in more detail.

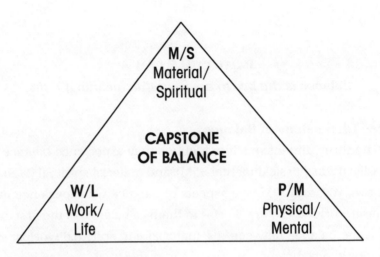

Work/Life Balance

For the purposes of our discussion, "work" must be defined to include the role of homemaker. Many households continue to divide the responsibilities between homemaker and breadwinner and both are full-time jobs. "Life," on the other hand, represents friends, family, and interests we pursue outside our work responsibilities. W/L balance is achieved when we're able to invest in both areas equally and experience a sense of satisfaction and connection with both.

Regardless of whether we're part of a household in which both spouses work, and the responsibilities are split, or we're single parents, most find W/L balance is difficult to attain. The difficulty goes back to a fundamental theme of the book, which is awareness. Most of us are fundamentally blind to the fact that we're completely in control of our W/L balance over the long term. Instead, many feel trapped in a state of imbalance, with work usually taking the lion's share of the time, effort, and attention.

A telltale sign we're living out of W/L balance is when we yield that control to someone or something else and claim that we are incapable of living in W/L balance. I say "long term" because we all experience times where we must do extra work or when personal issues force us to put our work on hold. However, over the long term, we're completely in control of our W/L balance. Whenever I hear someone relinquishing control to an unreasonable boss or job, I can't help but believe that person is unwilling to face the truth.

Why is it that we so often feel out of control in this area?

Culture of work:

The American Work Ethic is part of our national identity, and we're not alone. All over the globe, societies and countries emphasize work above nearly all else. Such an emphasis challenges our ability to maintain a W/L balance.

The world of investment banking has a reputation for long hours; working late into the night and on weekends is the norm. It also has a reputation for paying extraordinary sums of money in salaries and bonuses. Although I work for a regional bank that isn't a part of the Wall Street norm of seven-figure bonus payouts, my firm does emphasize work above all else and pays its people attractive bonuses for bringing in business. This same commitment to work is felt in most jobs and careers regardless of industry—but at what cost?

It's the rare company that understands the long-term implications of employees lacking a reasonable W/L balance. Many companies are managed on a short-term basis—from quarter to quarter—which obscures the long-term costs associated with W/L imbalance. There is an invisible but very real cost to the employees, and as a result, to the company for the "work-at-all-costs" approach.

Multiple studies have been conducted by the Ford Foundation, Ernst & Young, and the United States government to determine the impact of employee-friendly services such as child care, flexible hours, and working from home. The results are compelling. The companies that focus on providing flexibility and perks have far less turnover than those businesses that do not. It's also interesting to note that many employers who are interviewed regarding W/L-balance programs overwhelmingly believe that they work. There are a few key issues, however, that stand in the way of widespread acceptance of extensive W/L programs. These issues are senior leadership acceptance and the invisible cost of turnover.

Senior leadership acceptance:

Meaningful changes to a company's W/L balance programs must come from the top down. In the short run, these programs result in measurable costs in the form of time off, technology expense, and/or management training. These short-term costs will yield the long-term benefits of fewer turnovers and a happier, more productive workforce; however, the investment must come first. Without senior leadership support, these programs tend to be the first to go when times are tough financially. It takes a great deal of courage and commitment to see a program through difficult times.

Senior leadership support must come in the form of greater training at the middle-management level to effectively implement these programs. Old habits die hard, and many middle managers may have a negative bias against these new flexible work options. If key managers don't embrace the new work paradigm, many employees will be hesitant to take advantage of the program for fear of being excluded from promotions or raises. Any company must have the strong support of senior leadership to create lasting change.

Invisible cost of turnover:

Employee turnover is one of the most expensive, but least measured metrics in business. A recent Ernst & Young study on employee turnover quantified its cost to be 154 percent of the average compensation of the employee who left. Think about that number for a minute—154 percent! To make it more meaningful, let's compare two companies with $10 million of annual employee costs. Company A has turnover of 20 percent and Company B has turnover of 40 percent. Company A's turnover cost would be $1,080,000, while Company B's turnover cost would be twice that at $2,160,000. That represents an increase in employee costs of 10.8 percent for Company A and 21.6 percent for Company B without net new employees!

Often, companies feel they need to cut employees to create savings, which in turn creates even less employee satisfaction and results in further turnover. Instead of exclusive focus on sales and capital expenses, companies would be better served to drill down on their employee turnover metrics. They would find a nearly invisible human capital expense that, with attention, could be cut dramatically.

Our responsibility:

Ultimately, W/L balance is our responsibility. I knew that a career in investment banking would mean a position with longer hours and higher stress than many jobs from which I could choose. As long as I value the compensation more than the higher potential for W/L balance, I will continue to pursue a career in banking. But while in banking, there is a great deal I can control. I can take my kids with me on an annual trip. I can take Kim to one of my conferences. I can manage my workload such that I spend time with my family in the early evening and go back to work when they go to bed. These are choices I can make for more effective W/L balance. In the long term, I have even more choices, including a lower-stress position outside of banking.

Some companies are better to work for than others. *Fortune* provides an annual list of the top 100 companies to work for and tallies the features that make them unique. No company is perfect, but many on the list do a better job than most in creating a flexible, worker-friendly environment. But these companies, and others like them, can only lay the foundation or framework for improved W/L balance. Most of the imbalance in our jobs or careers results from a self-imposed inability to leave work at work. Whether motivated by fear, ambition, or greed, more work is thought to be better than less. However, it's vital we make the most of our lives outside of work so that we may enjoy a rich, multi-dimensional life.

A Personal Example

My wife can tell you about many times when my personal drive and ambition have been inappropriately transferred to her. One recent example had to do with our move into our dream house. Finances were tight because the house payment was a significant step up from our previous payment, *plus* we still owned our other house. I was concerned about our financial situation and started talking to Kim about getting a job. She had more than ten years of experience as a corporate banker and had very marketable skills. Thankfully, our house sold before she was forced to seriously consider joining the workplace.

I, of course, didn't let the topic of her starting a new job go. I had all kinds of reasons for her to want to rejoin the workforce. The extra money would be helpful with the expense of our new house. Our kids' 529 accounts for college could be bigger. On and on, I reasoned. But my real issue, deep down inside, was a belief that Kim should want to go to work. Why didn't she have any desire to work? Where was her discipline and work ethic?

My pressing on these issues resulted in emotional and painful discussions with tears of frustration. I finally stopped pushing the issue and after a couple of months, I had a personal revelation about it. Kim is an excellent wife, mother, and homemaker. She genuinely enjoys the challenge and rewards of being a stay-at-home mom. Even though she never told me this, she has another very personal reason for wanting to be a homemaker. Her mom died when she was ten years old and Kim had to make do with no one at home. Her dad was able to keep her in many school activities with the help of friends and family, but it wasn't the same as having a mother. She never wanted that to be the case with our kids.

I began to realize how difficult it is for women to deal with the conflicting goals society places on them. It's not enough to be a mom; you have to be a mom with a career. Or for the working mothers, you're somehow cheating your family for wanting your own career. At the heart of these decisions is a struggle for balance. For Kim, her decision was difficult, but the right choice for her. I feel for those families who are struggling for their own sense of balance in their uniquely personal situations. This is but one example of the W/L balance decisions we must make. The key is to become cognizant of how our decisions impact our balance daily—especially in regard to life-changing decisions.

Physical/Mental Balance

The other cornerstone at the foundation of the pyramid's capstone is P/M balance. Like W/L balance, P/M balance, when achieved, allows us to move more freely into M/S balance. As I researched P/M balance, I found a significant number of studies confirming what most of us already know—the link between physical and mental health is indisputable. For example, Duke University did a study in which patients with severe depression were divided into three groups. The first group received the anti-depressant Zoloft; the second group got Zoloft along with a modest exercise program (thirty minutes, three times a week); and the third was prescribed only the modest exercise program. A year later, the group that had performed best was the exercise-only group. Those who had taken Zoloft had higher depression relapse rates.[25] Isn't it interesting that the drugs many consider necessary for treatment of depression may not be needed at all?

Another study confirmed this result: loneliness impairs the immune system.[26] What I found fascinating about this study was that some of the patients were more isolated than others, however, those who were isolated had to *feel* as though they were lonely. Many, in fact, did not feel lonely. In contrast, there were many who had a wide circle of friends, but felt lonely anyway.

Numerous studies have been done regarding stress and its impact on the body and the immune system. Stress (a type of mental dysfunction) had a significant negative impact on the physical health of those participating in the study—particularly on those who didn't also exercise. Clearly, exercise does more than keep off unwanted pounds; it improves our mental health in ways we're only beginning to understand.

I'm absolutely convinced that my commitment to a regular exercise routine has helped limit the impact of work stress. Exercise helps provide an outlet for the tension, fear, and worry of everyday life. Many scientists believe that the release of endorphins during and after exercise provides the relief from stress, but I think that's only part of the story. For me, exercise has become a form of meditation where I focus on the exercise, the breathing and, when I am at my best, nothing else.

To expand on a topic we have discussed earlier, awareness of the mind's ongoing dialogue is crucial. Exercise is an activity that can allow

[25] James A. Blumenthal et. al. "Effects of Exercise Training on Older Patients with Major Depression," *Archives of Internal Medicine*, October 25, 1999.

[26] Sarah D. Pressman et. al. "Loneliness, Social Network Size and Immune Response to Influenza Vaccination in College Freshmen," *University of Rochester: Health Psychology*, Vol. 24, No. 3.

gaps or stillness in the stream of thinking originating from our Judging Mind or ego. These gaps in thinking allow for a greater awareness of the Natural Self. When we connect with the Natural Self, we create a pathway out of the material world and into the spiritual.

By exercising, we accomplish two objectives. First, we improve physical health. A consistent exercise program will result in improved strength, a more healthy weight, and a reduction in stress through the release of endorphins. Second, and even more important, our exercise program can be a form of meditation to quiet the mind. Focusing on the physical activity alone and using meditation techniques such as following our breathing, we bring mental stillness into the routine.

Many Eastern cultures have taken this connection between the mind and body to the next level by creating specific forms of exercise that further enhance the benefits of the physical on the mental. Exercises found in yoga and tai chi reduce stress by a focus on more than just the physical. Both have moved into the mainstream, with such prestigious Western health organizations as the Mayo Clinic and the Cleveland Clinic recognizing their therapeutic benefits.

For more information on yoga and tai chi, check your local gym or fitness center for classes or teachers. Neither requires specific licensing, so check several sources and request references. Ultimately, you should choose an exercise routine that works for you in accomplishing the objectives of physical conditioning and quieting the mind.

Material/Spiritual Balance

W/L and P/M balance are at the foundation of the balance capstone. At its top is M/S balance. As we achieve greater balance in the W/L and P/M areas of our lives, we become better prepared for the summit of the pyramid: M/S balance.

In the introduction of this book, I said of this summit that, "The oxygen is a bit thin up there." Since most of us spend more time in the material world than the spiritual world, we must recognize the difficulty in maintaining perfect balance between these realms. The goal is to spend more time at the summit striving for the peace and serenity of God while being a light to others. However, our lives in the material world can't be ignored and replaced by the spiritual world. We must constantly strive for balance to live life to the fullest. Here are some examples.

Practice forgiveness:

In Chapter Five, I mentioned that forgiveness is an act of love done more for the forgiver than for the forgiven. When we're consumed with hate and resentment rather than love and forgiveness, we hurt ourselves far more than the object of our hatred. Forgiveness is a theme running throughout the Bible. Jesus says, "If you hold anything against anyone, forgive him, so that your Father in heaven may forgive you your sins" (Mark 11:25, NIV). Forgiveness is a principle that transcends the material world and becomes a part of the spiritual world.

As we strive to practice forgiveness, it's important not to blindly check the "I forgive" box on our spiritual checklist. Forgiveness takes effort, consideration, and balance between the material and the spiritual worlds. We must be able to "forgive the sinner, but not the sin."

If we have a friend or colleague who is spreading false or nasty rumors about us or our families, our first reaction is likely to be anger or hatred. Forgiveness is the last thing on our minds. Although we may realize that retribution is the wrong path, our ego has been hurt and our strong desire may be to hurt the other person in return. What if we just forgive the person right then and there without conversation or confrontation? Is that living at a higher level of M/S balance? The answer is probably not. If we aren't willing to confront the other person, we're likely hiding behind a façade of self-piety. The ego's defense becomes one of, "I'm too evolved to stoop to the level of the other person's ill will and bad taste."

In reality, the more evolved person may well be the one willing to confront the friend in an objective and non-threatening way. Forgiveness is the true path toward peace and better M/S balance; however, we must have the courage to confront others and articulate how their sins will not be tolerated. As this example underscores, the subtleties of balance between the material and spiritual worlds requires that we be nimble, flexible, and willing to operate at our highest personal levels.

Parenting challenges:

As a father, I'm constantly reminded of the challenge of M/S balance in raising children. New challenges exist at each stage of childhood, and my wife and I are only beginning to confront what many tell me is the greatest challenge of all: the teenage years. I can see how our decisions as parents will have lasting impact on our children as they enter adulthood. Freedom from parents and a nearly myopic focus on the material aspects of life will begin to dominate a child's thought process as he enters middle school. Peer pressure regarding phones, clothes, and all other material things become of primary concern. Social networks and fitting in with a group become much more important than attending church or donating time to a worthy cause. As parents, it's important that we pick our spots and stay firm on the big issues. Some examples might be a mission trip through church, donating time to the local food pantry, or other areas of importance to your family and community.

Pick your spots, but stay firm on the big issues.

As our kids confront the pressures of our materialistic and consumer oriented society it's vital they have the life experiences of giving of themselves for someone else's benefit. A foundation built on sound principles will allow them to navigate through the pitfalls of greed and the bondage of debt that most of us inevitably encounter. And we can't expect them to be people of honor and integrity just because we tell them to be. We have to model integrity of thought and deed every day in the way we live. Children can spot hypocritical behavior faster than most adults.

As we balance our children's desire of more freedom with our own desire to limit their mistakes, we must recognize that only they can live their lives. Their journey will be just as unique as our own, and although we may provide our wisdom from experience, they must travel their own paths. As I look at my own childhood, I recognize how focused I was on material and financial success. It was only much later that I began to realize I was missing a big part of my true Natural Self.

As much as I hope my life experience will provide wisdom to help my children through the challenges of our material world, I pray that my real legacy will be in bringing a spiritual awareness to them. They will eventually realize the limits of the material world and I want them to have enough exposure to the depth of the spiritual world for it to be a resource for continued growth.

Perfect balance:

There's an old Chinese saying that every stick (or life) has two ends: a material end and a spiritual end. As we grow older, the stick grows in proportion to our age. The center of the stick represents perfect balance between the material and spiritual worlds.

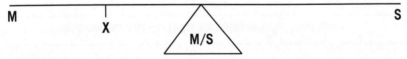

In today's world, the overwhelming tendency is to invest time and effort in the material side of life while ignoring the spiritual side. This creates a perpetual feeling of being out of balance. Rather than abiding at the mid-point of the line, we live at a different point beyond balance

(X). Unfortunately, the material cues from society trick us into investing more and more into the material with a promise of finding peace and harmony waiting at that next milestone.

But peace and harmony never come and we move on from one mirage to the next trying to find them. Although many realize the folly in this single-minded pursuit, the realization often comes too late. The earlier we can recognize imbalance, the better equipped we are to make significant changes. Giving of ourselves to others in the form of our time, talent, and treasure are an investment into the spiritual side of life. Additionally, time spent in meditation and prayer deepens our spiritual dimension.

Have you ever wondered why at the end of his life a dying man scrambles to give away what he has so painstakingly accumulated over the years? Perhaps he's seen the light that material wealth can't be taken to the grave. How much more joy would he have enjoyed if he had spent more of his life giving of himself to others. If the only way we invest in the spiritual side of life is by creating a charitable foundation when we die, we're only cheating ourselves. We all have a material and a spiritual side to life; both are vitally important. Seek truth and awareness of how you're balancing these in your life.

Like so many great truths, it's at once very simple and yet one of life's greatest challenges. When we're living in balance we're at the pinnacle of successful, disciplined living. A life in balance is full of confidence, peace, and tranquility.

Key Takeaways:

1. Balance is the key to living at the highest level. When we operate in balance, we're successfully utilizing the tools of discipline: delayed gratification, personal responsibility, and dedication to the truth.

2. The balance capstone has W/L and P/M at the foundation— balances of the first order. M/S is at the top of the capstone—

balance of the second order.

3. W/L balance requires awareness of our behavior and a willingness to change.

4. Our work-dominated society makes W/L balance difficult to achieve; however, we're responsible for making the changes needed to achieve it.

5. The physical and the mental are linked. A lack of health in one area can have negative implications for the other.

6. Exercise does far more than improve physical health. It also improves mental health through an intense focus on the physical coupled with a quieting of the mind.

7. Yoga and tai chi are designed to quiet the mind and challenge the body. This type of exercise does as much for mental health as it does for physical health.

8. M/S balance requires us to live effectively in both the material and spiritual worlds. Blindly checking the "forgiveness box" when we're mistreated may only serve to strengthen our ego. We must forgive the sinner, but not the sin.

9. Our children are confronted with a material-dominated world. It's our responsibility to introduce spiritual truths as part of their development.

10. Life can be represented by a stick with two ends: the material and the spiritual. We only achieve balance in our lives when both areas receive equal time and attention.

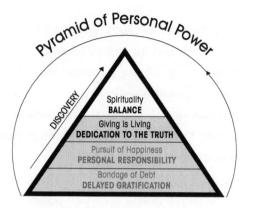

CHAPTER 9

SPIRITUAL MINDSET

"Still runnin,' I'm still runnin' against the wind."
– Bob Seeger

Until recently, I've felt a kinship with Bob Seeger's classic song *Against the Wind*. It was as if the lyrics were written for me and my struggles with life's challenges. The lyrics resonated with me as part of the American Dream of struggle and hard work in order to "make it." Although it's inevitable that we'll face resistance, we don't have to do so alone or without faith. Why is it then that so many of us feel we're constantly running against the wind all by ourselves? Why are peace and faith so fleeting?

As we discovered in previous chapters, most of the challenges we face are of our own creation. Our Judging Mind is often so fearful, so condemning of our failings or setbacks that we unwittingly communicate to our natural or subconscious mind that we are not good enough. These feelings of lack have a profoundly negative effect on our ability to live a happy, fulfilled life. They also keep us from achieving our personal goals.

The only way to reach our personal goals while not being thwarted by running against the wind is through a spiritual mindset. A spiritual mindset is the opposite of a judging mindset. A spiritual mindset replaces self-doubt and condemnation with faith and peace. But faith may only be built on a strong spiritual foundation. I must be clear about two points here. First, the previous chapters describe the work needed on a personal level to develop faith in self. Although vitally important, faith in self only brings us part way to inner peace and self-actualization. Equally important is faith in a power beyond ourselves. I think of it in this way; faith in self allows us to make incremental changes to improve how we interact with others or "get ahead" in our careers, whereas faith in a higher power allows us to make quantum leaps in our personal development. Spiritual faith gives us the strength to operate at a level far beyond where our existing "comfort zones" might allow us to grow.

Second, belief in a higher power does not provide us with a "lottery ticket" to life. We still must do our part to achieve personal success or inner peace and live a balanced life. We must do everything we can to achieve our goals and then leave the rest up to God, faith, and love.

This chapter explores techniques to bring us closer to God and build up a spiritual mindset. A developed spiritual mindset brings a sense of faith and inner peace regarding our lives and reduces the worry we may be confronting on a daily basis. Faith is a muscle that must be exercised to become stronger. These faith-building exercises are easy and rewarding, but very often overlooked as we become consumed in the material world. However, to build a stronger faith, they must be practiced regularly.

Prayer

Scheduling time to pray every day is an important first step. Many people do not pray because they feel awkward in prayer—almost as if the prayer needs to sound like a verse from the King James Bible. This could not be further from the truth! God wants to hear from us in a familiar way. We should speak with God as though he is our Friend sitting right next to us. Also, it's important to be thankful in prayer—to thank him for our many blessings even though we might have some troubles we want to share as well. Thankful prayer reminds us of all the gifts God has already given us. In addition, affirmative prayer thanks God for things we may not yet have and creates a sense of positive expectancy.

One of the most compelling believers in prayer was the Reverend Norman Vincent Peale who wrote many books, including his landmark bestseller, *The Power of Positive Thinking*. In that book, Dr. Peale discusses the merits of prayer in both scientific and spiritual terms in his folksy, conversational style:

> Personally, I believe that prayer is a sending out of vibrations from one person to another and to God. The entire universe is in vibration. When we send out a prayer for another person, we employ the force inherent in a spiritual universe. We transport from ourselves to other people a sense of love, helpfulness, support—a sympathetic, powerful under-standing—and in this process we awaken vibrations in the universe through which God brings to pass the good objectives prayed for.[27]

Be positive:

When speaking with God, we should be positive in our words, affirm the many things we already have and that we wish to receive.

Affirmation of the gifts we want to receive lays the groundwork for achieving our prayers.

---

[27] Norman Vincent Peale, *The Power of Positive Thinking* (New York: Prentice Hall, 1952), pg. 48.

Affirmation of the gifts we want to receive lays the groundwork for achieving our prayers. For example, I prayed about the writing of this book. I was concerned that I would not be able to complete it due to the other substantial commitments in my life. I have a full-time job as a banker; I'm a father to two children; and I have a wonderful, supportive wife. All of these areas of life are important to me and I did not want to sacrifice any of them to write the book. However, the book was important to me as well. So, every day, twice a day I prayed about the book. My prayer when something like this: "Thank you God for planting a seed of desire in my heart for writing this book. I know that by nourishing this seed, I will be able to write a compelling book, while continuing to be a good father, husband, and employee."

This affirmative prayer brought a sense of calmness and resolve into my life. I was affirming a faith in God that I would be able to write this book without sacrificing key relationships, and to a large degree I was able to do it. (The primary sacrifice was not watching as much TV or playing as much golf.)

Pray often:

Before I fully appreciating the power of prayer, my prayer time was quite limited. I would pray while at church (when I attended, that is), or I might pray at night if something was going on in my life that I was particularly anxious about. My prayer at church helped me to relax and decompress, but my prayer at night was often a pleading, begging sort of prayer, which, as I look back on it, was not based in faith. Praying from a mindset of lack only magnifies the lack; however, praying an affirmative, thankful prayer creates a sense of gratitude and underscores the many prayers already answered in our lives.

Praying in this way has the dual purposes of reminding us of life's many blessings as well as building our faith in good things to come. I now pray at least twice a day—in the morning before work and in the evening before bed. Because I find prayer so renewing, I often pray many other times during the day: in the car, on the plane, etc. I know of no better way to express gratitude and calm fear than faithful prayer. It's taken my most stressful days and made them far easier. My wife says I'm more relaxed and, probably most important for me, I'm not nearly as quick to anger as I used to be.

Pray for others:

Do you pray for others? Perhaps you say a prayer for family members or friends. These prayers are extremely important as they allow us to touch those most important to us, which gives us a sense of appreciation and peace for having these people in our lives. I encourage everyone to take prayer for others a step further by praying for those you do not know. Perhaps you see someone on a plane who looks down or who's struggling with an unruly child. Maybe you see someone on the news who is facing a personal disaster. Send these strangers your prayers. It creates a sense of peace within you, but it also impacts those people in ways we're only beginning to realize. The most challenging form of prayer for me personally is praying for those who have hurt me in some way.

In order to enjoy peace in our lives, we must learn the power of forgiveness. Forgiveness is a recurring theme in the Bible, including being part of the Lord's Prayer: "Forgive us our trespasses, as we forgive those who trespass against us" (see Matthew 6:12 and Luke 11:4). Many people think that forgiveness is done for the benefit of the person who "trespassed against us." That's not true! Forgiveness is for us. Here's why: Jesus wants us to forgive those who trespass against us to bring peace into our lives. Resentment and hate bring nothing but poison.

Praying for others who hurt us removes bitterness from our hearts.

Think about a recent situation where somebody wronged you or did something that was extremely hurtful. Have you forgiven that person? When you think of the offense, does it still bring rage or resentment? If so, you have not forgiven that person and you continue to carry bitterness around with you.

I remember such an example with my sister, Debbie. My sister and her family live in a nearby community in Atlanta. She had just moved to a new home and had gone to visit some friends in Florida right after the move. My mom was watching her two kids and I suggested that we come over with our kids to see the house and give her a break. My mom informed me, however, that she was under strict orders not to let us see the house before my sister had a chance to give us the grand tour. Evidently Debbie had planned a gathering at her house and did not want us to come before then.

I thought this was a silly and selfish request. When my sister came back to town I told her I thought it was selfish of her to not allow us to visit before the gathering. I said it would have been a nice break for Mom. Her reply was curt and cutting: "Well, you don't have to come to the house at all." I was shocked, hurt, and angered simultaneously. As I look back on it now, I can understand why she wanted to be the one to show us the new house; it was her new house. She was proud of it. She wanted to see our reaction. At the time, however, I resented her retort to my admonishments. I was so taken off-guard, I did not know what to say and felt a deep sense of anger. I wanted to tell her that it was her prerogative whether or not we visited. How petty of me!

My kids were so excited to come to the house, and I needed to swallow my pride and stick with the plan. However, that phone conversation with my sister ate away at me for months. I resented her putting me in that position, all for what I considered to be pride and selfishness. I'm sure you can think of times when your family caused a similar sense of anger and frustration. Have you let it eat away at you and strain relationships like I did with my sister? Have you delayed forgiveness thinking that it's the other person's fault? Consider the Lord's Prayer and realize that withholding forgiveness only destroys your sense of peace and well-being. Life is too short for this type of thinking.

Think of someone who has recently hurt you. You can start with a big or a small issue; just pick something that's eating away at you and creating bitterness. Pray for that person. Forgive that person. It's the only way you will be able to live in peace and harmony. Roots of bitterness only hurt us, not the other person.

Roots of bitterness only hurt us.

Meditation

It's often said that praying is speaking to God and meditating is listening to God. We're all aware of the importance of listening. It's the foundation for good communication with our colleagues, friends, and family. Adding meditation to my daily prayer routine has been a challenging yet rewarding experience for me. Just as listening to others is sometimes a challenge, listening to God and our hearts is a challenge. There are thousands of books about the methods, history, and roots of meditation. To these I will add my description of how meditation can assist us in being still, listening to our hearts, and feeling the Spirit of God within us.

Praying is speaking to God; meditation is listening to God.

Just like a child can pick up a ball, bat, and glove and play baseball with very little practice, so you and I can begin practicing meditation without any formal training. Like playing ball, meditation is very easy; however, refining and improving our skill in meditation is a journey that never ends. Just as an athlete practices and trains to master the skills of his sport, meditation requires the same level of focus and training. Let's explore the purpose, process, and benefits of meditation.

Purpose:

The discipline of meditation quiets the mind. Have you noticed that during the day, your mind jumps from one topic to the next? You're having multiple conversations with yourself about various topics and this constant dialogue makes it very difficult to focus. One of the first things we do with meditation is work on quieting the mind. Once the mind is quiet, we are better able to concentrate on the task at hand. The ability to focus exclusively on the task at hand may seem to be a very elementary goal, but it's fundamental to doing anything well. Think of the most skilled athletes: LeBron James, Derek Jeter, or Roger Federer. What separates them from other skilled players is their ability to focus on their tasks better than just about everyone else. It's this concentration that allows them to excel.

Once we quiet the mind through the discipline of meditation, we're able to listen. By listening, I mean we become more receptive or open to the desires of our heart, the nature of our soul, and the wisdom of God. This receptivity can only take place when the mind is quiet, and even then may come in small steps as we journey down the path of meditation. I've been meditating for more than three years and I am only just now catching glimpses of the power brought about through meditation. The interesting thing with meditation is that the more we seek this wisdom, the more fleeting it seems.

As we become more skilled at meditation, we'll begin to have better insight into our true selves. This improved insight allows us to handle setbacks, challenges, and questions that arise in everyday life. Perhaps most importantly, skilled meditation allows us to achieve an inner peace, reduce stress, and remain calm in trying situations.

Process:

I meditate twice a day for ten to twenty minutes. Sometimes I meditate just prior to prayer and other times I meditate just after, but in all cases I combine prayer and meditation into a twenty-to-thirty minute period of quiet just before bed in the evening and prior to work first thing in the morning. The first, and most difficult, step for me is quieting my mind. When I first began meditating, I was under the wrong impression that meditation meant thinking of nothing— emptying the mind completely. I was not having success as my mind wandered from one topic to the next. Ultimately, I discovered that the mind must focus on something. Quieting the mind does not mean thinking of nothing; it means focusing our attention on one thing. This ability to focus is one of the keys to successful meditation.

Most books on the topic suggest focusing on our breathing by either counting breaths or noticing the actual process of breathing. In and out, we begin to relax by counting breaths. The mind will try to wander, but we must gently bring it back to the process of breathing. Do not be judgmental as the mind wanders; just bring it back gently to your breathing.

Early on, I found this to be extremely difficult. All kinds of silly thoughts ran through my mind: my calendar for the next day, a news story, or even what I had for lunch. The key is to stay with it until we begin to feel light, calm and in the groove of the meditation. Sometimes when I find my mind wandering uncontrollably, I will use spiritual phrases to quiet it. Some of my favorites include:

- Trust in God
- Peace, love, and happiness
- I am divinely led
- Walk the path of God

These phrases focus the mind on something without disrupting the meditation. There you have it! You're beginning to meditate without formal training. I too am a mere beginner with much to learn about how to maximize my meditative experience. However, many of the benefits may be realized early on regardless of our experience level.

Benefits:

Although I'm early in my meditation training, I've already begun to see benefits. The key benefit is a calmer, more relaxed state of mind. It was subtle at first, but over the last few years, my demeanor has changed. I'm not so quick to anger, and I stop to see things that before I never would have paid attention to, like pine trees against an evening sky, or the way they sway back and forth with the breeze, or the subtle noises of my back yard full of birds, crickets, and other living things. I'm spending more time smelling the roses, and I'm more patient with my kids, my wife, and even myself.

Prior to meditating, I used sleep aids to get to sleep about half the time. Since I began meditating and praying, I rarely have to take anything for sleep. Meditation and prayer in the evening is the perfect way for me to unwind and close the day. The process of thankful prayer and meditation in the evening prepares the body for rest by clearing the mind while thanking God for my blessings.

In 1972, Herbert Benson, a renowned cardiologist, wrote a book titled *The Relaxation Response*. Dr. Benson approached the value of meditation from a scientific perspective to underscore the amazing health benefits of meditation. At the time the book was written, meditation was relatively novel; it was an Eastern practice largely unknown in the United States. Dr. Benson outlined a specific meditation process in the book, which I found compelling. But I also believe the mechanics of meditation can be tailored to the interests and the desires of the individual.

The essence of Benson's book was to spotlight the physical benefits of meditation. It relaxes the body, lowers the heart rate, and eliminates the physical and mental tension that can cause heart disease and hypertension. I see the physical benefits as icing on the cake of the mental well-being, focus, and relaxation that meditation produces in our lives. I'm much more relaxed in my job and better able to handle the inevitable challenges that come up. I approach the day with a relaxed ease unlike anything I had before. I did not quiet my mind; instead, my concerns and worries began in the shower and traveled with me to work.

Now, I begin my day by reading three chapters in the Bible and considering its wisdom and applicability to my day. Then I meditate and pray with a more thankful and relaxed heart. I find it difficult to have a bad day when I start this way. It takes me about forty minutes and I look forward to my communion with God first thing in the morning. I've found nothing better!

Reading the Bible

My girlfriend in college gave me a Bible early on in our relationship. Even though it was a New International Version translation (which many find easier to read the King James translation), every time I picked it up to read something for a Sunday school class or just for personal growth, I got stuck right away. I allowed the customs and language of the day to become an impediment to my understanding and enjoyment.

I freely admit that I gave up too quickly because the Bible is filled with inspirational and practical wisdom for everyday living. It wasn't until I was much older that I became inspired to try reading the Bible again. A number of factors and events drew me back to the Bible, almost as if God was working through people and circumstances to awake the desire within me to begin reading again.

The process:

To successfully read the Bible, I felt I needed to do two things. First, I needed to break it up into small, easy to handle pieces. I did not want to discourage myself by taking on whole books at one sitting. Second, I needed a guide to help me understand some of the key principles and ways in which I could apply those principles in my life.

To accomplish the first goal, I decided to read three chapters a day. The second goal was accomplished by purchasing a study Bible[28] which included some interpretation of the verses and notes on how to apply the teachings into daily life. I incorporated my Bible study into my morning routine: first by reading the three chapters, next by reading the commentary, and finally by meditating and praying about what I'd read. This takes me thirty to forty-five minutes depending on the readings and the reflection.

This daily ritual has improved my outlook considerably. Before beginning my day this way, I would bring a mind full of concern and worry to work with me. By beginning with reflection on God's word along with thankful prayer and meditation, those worries and fears are replaced by faith and thankfulness. I firmly believe this reflection on the Bible and its core principles of faith and love is the best way to begin each day. It's been a subtle transition, but I'm far more relaxed and composed after investing this time first thing in the morning.

Bible study group:

Joining a Bible study group can expand your knowledge and be a great way to meet people with a similar desire to better understand the

---

[28] *The Everyday Life Bible* with commentary by Joyce Meyer. It is the Amplified Bible translation. I found the parenthetical alternative definitions within the body of the Bible somewhat distracting; however, Joyce's commentary was extremely beneficial and helped me relate many of the difficult-to-interpret passages to my everyday life. There are numerous other companion guides that can be used as part of your Bible reading and I highly recommend you find something to help you learn.

word of God. Ideally, you'll want to find a Bible study affiliated with your church. This is an excellent way to get to know people who attend your church, while developing closer ties within your church community. If there isn't a convenient Bible study group affiliated with your church, seek out alternatives at work or in the community. The goal is to find Christians seeking to better understand and relate Scripture to their daily lives. You may need to try two or more groups before finding the right fit.

You may ask, "What's the goal?" I believe relating the Bible to daily life is a core goal. To make Scripture a living document, we must strive to "live the document." That doesn't mean we'll all be perfect Christians. I'm certain I've only begun to walk the path of complete faith in God. To become more faithful, we must incorporate what the Bible teaches into our own development.

To make Scripture a living document, we must strive to
"live the document."

Scripture in action:

To make the Bible relevant, consider writing down passages that resonate, and think about how Scripture relates to your everyday life. The Bible has timeless wisdom that reveals itself when studied more closely. Here are a few verses along with their meaning to me:

"A tree is recognized by its fruit" (Matthew 12:33, NIV).

Your thoughts have a powerful determination on your ultimate results in life. How do you feel about yourself? You are a unique gift from God! There is no one else like you on earth! Thank God for the unique strengths that make you different from all others. Take your strengths and use them for good. It's not enough to be at peace with yourself and God; you must reach out and extend yourself through love to help others. Bear your unique fruit as a gift to others.

"Gains the whole world and forfeits his soul" (Matthew 16:26, NIV). How many of us are envious of those who make a lot of money, have significant fame, or are gifted athletes? Material winnings are only a small part of what any of us are. Remember, none of our material gains may be taken with us when we die. To truly be a peace, we must live our lives with discipline of heart and integrity of action. So many of these people who become icons of wealth or fame end up as alcoholics, divorced, and unhappy. Gaining the whole "material world" at the expense of your soul is too high a price to pay. Living a life of faith and integrity, while not making headlines, will bring you infinitely more blessings in the long run. Think about how your life can make a lasting impact on others through your leadership and actions.

"Unless you change and become like little children, you will never enter the kingdom of heaven" (Matthew 18:3, NIV). As adults, it's so beautiful to see the simple and pure faith of our children. As we grow older, the ability to believe or have faith in a higher power often fades. Our faith becomes obscured by the realities of life. The point that I take from this Scripture is that faith and belief are core to becoming true Christians. We must believe in the presence of God in our lives to enter heaven. Faith and belief also bring us peace, which is as close to heaven as we will ever be on earth.

"If anyone wants to be first, he must be the very last, and the servant of all" (Mark 9:35, NIV). I was extremely fortunate to have a mentor early in my career who truly embodied what Jesus meant here. Walker Choppin was my manager for the first four years of my career as a banker. Walker managed about six of us in the healthcare group. Due in large part to Walker's creativity and relationships within the healthcare community, our group was extremely profitable for the bank, and of course, he was extremely busy. Aside from his skills and knowledge as a banker, what so impressed me about Walker was how generous he was with his time for anyone who needed his help. As the newest banker of the group, I needed a great deal of help. He gave me freedom to work on transactions on my own, but he was always available to help strategize on structure, sales strategy, and internal approval. He would stay late to help me when I knew he was tired and wanted to be home with his family. All the while, he was generous with the credit for winning the deal. Walker's servant leadership was an excellent example for me at the beginning of my career and I will always be grateful for his generosity of spirit. I am just one of many whose lives and careers he touched and he will always be an inspiration to me and to all the others whom he impacted through his servant leadership.

Entering the Spiritual Realm

When you take time to pray, meditate, and reflect on Scripture, you will find the muscle of faith strengthened. Strong faith helps bring peace despite the numerous challenges of everyday life. It's easy to get caught up in the current crisis or to get lost in thought as we try to solve life's problems; however, those who develop a practice of meditation, prayer, and Scripture reading find deeper meanings through life's challenges. Even if it means creating the space that allows us to hang on just a little longer when encountering a very difficult situation, these tools help us to solve problems that we cannot solve alone. They equip us to enter what I call life's spiritual realm.

Within the spiritual realm, we have access to wisdom and solutions to problems beyond our own skills and knowledge alone. It's impossible to simply decide, "I'm going to access the wisdom of the ages and enter the spiritual realm." All we can do is become open to this wisdom through the tools described in this chapter. Once we become receptive to wisdom beyond our own understanding, the answers to life's difficult problems often shows up by grace through all sorts of channels:

Message at church. Whether you attend church regularly or not, think about a time when you attended and found that the minister's message focused on an issue you happened to be struggling with at that very moment. Do you remember the sense of surprise? Did you find yourself focused on the message in a way that you hadn't been during past messages?

Call from a friend. What about the time you received a call from someone you were thinking about the day or night before. You may have been worried about that person or just wondering how they were doing. Perhaps they needed to hear from you to get through a tough situation—were you there for them?

Serendipity. It was a late night flight home many years ago. At the time I was struggling with my Christian faith. I didn't have anything to read, so I checked the seat-back pocket for the in-flight magazine. There was a paperback book in the pocket titled *Mere Christianity* by C. S. Lewis. I recognized Lewis as the author of *The Lion, the Witch, and the Wardrobe*, but I wasn't familiar with his numerous writings as a Christian scholar. The book was exactly what I needed to rekindle my faith.

Most would write the above off as coincidences and not think about them after the fact. But what if "coincidences" were instances where the spiritual realm intersected with our material world? Rather than coincidences, I believe these to be guideposts from God. These guideposts are everywhere, but we're so lost in thought or focused on our material wants that they are lost on us. It's vital, therefore, to use the tools in this chapter to open ourselves up to these guideposts. With practice and a genuine desire to become open to the spiritual realm, we can find that which is most important to us.

I find spirituality to be a fleeting moment of awareness of the truth. Although fleeting and often obscured by our material desires, it is no less vital to our sense of well-being. Spirituality centers us on the most important things and we'll be the happiest and most fulfilled when we have a spiritual dimension to our lives. Spirituality doesn't mean we have all of the answers, but it recognizes that these answers exist in the universal truths we observe in life, both consciously and subconsciously.

Key Takeaways:

1. The power of faith allows us to make quantum leaps in our personal development. Faith encourages a partnership with God that stops our habit of "running against the wind."

2. Thankful prayer affirms what we wish to bring into our lives. We should speak to God as a friend; he wants to hear from us.

3. Pray at least twice a day: in the morning and in the evening. The discipline of prayer reminds us of our good fortune while replacing fear with peace and faith.

4. Pray for others, especially those who have harmed you in some way. Eliminate bitterness in your heart by forgiving the person through prayer.

5. Prayer is speaking to God and meditation is listening to God. Meditate at least twice a day, either before or after your prayer time.

6. The goal of meditation is to quiet the mind and relax. This calm awareness state may unlock thoughts that had previously been buried by the busy mind. Focus on breath or use a spiritual phrase to quiet the mind.

7. The benefits of meditation include: a more relaxed state that will improve our temperament and make us less susceptible to anger; a replacement of fear with faith; a reduction of stress; and improved physical health.

8. Read the Bible by breaking it up into manageable pieces. To better understand the Scripture, buy a study Bible or a companion text that clarifies scriptural teachings.

9. To do a better job of "living the document," we should write down verses that are meaningful in our personal journal that we can refer to in our free time—waiting for the bus, at the airport, etc.

10. The spiritual realm provides answers to life's most challenging problems, and is received by us as a gift (grace). Using the tools in this chapter will open us up to guideposts from God.

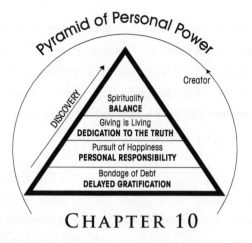

Pyramid of Personal Power

DISCOVERY

Creator

Spirituality
BALANCE

Giving is Living
DEDICATION TO THE TRUTH

Pursuit of Happiness
PERSONAL RESPONSIBILITY

Bondage of Debt
DELAYED GRATIFICATION

CHAPTER 10

THE CREATOR

"The world is but a canvas to the imagination."
– Henry David Thoreau

Each one of us has a driving need to be a creator deep inside, and when that desire isn't fulfilled we become dissatisfied. As creators we become focused, committed, and excited about our lives and experience a joy and satisfaction otherwise unattainable.

So what, you might ask, are the traits of a good creator? When we closely observe those whom we most admire for their creativity we see a common thread. First, the creative individual is actively engaged in a project, event, or hobby that is in sync with his or her guiding principles. As we learned in the Discovery chapter, each of us has unique interests, gifts, and guiding principles. We're at our best as creators when we're pursuing creative endeavors in sync with these guiding principles. Second, as creators, we become focused and engrossed in our creative activity.

The tools of discipline that are the framework of this book—delayed gratification, personal responsibility, dedication to the truth, and balance—are allies to the creative process. Rather than fighting against them, we embrace the tools to assist us as creators. Finally, we develop a passion for our creative endeavor. Joy and satisfaction accompany our creative activity and spark a passion for life. The mundane is replaced by curiosity, and work is replaced by focused engagement.

Ultimate Act

Perhaps the best example of creation—and the one most of us can relate to by the time we're forty—is having your first child. Do you remember the time, preparation, and effort you invested in becoming a new parent? I sure do. Kim and I bought books about pregnancy, birth, and the first year of the new child's life. We decorated the nursery with such care and attention to detail. I remember how much we struggled with decisions regarding the furniture and color schemes.

We made the decision to find out the sex of the baby (a boy), so we bought clothes and used colors in the nursery appropriate for a boy. And we were very blessed to have the family rally around the birth of our new son. My mom spent several weeks with us helping Kim and me enter a new world in which we had no experience. Kim's father, Jack, visited us from St. Louis to see his grandson and be a part of this new journey with us. The whole experience brought our family closer and gave us a renewed appreciation for the blessing of life. Challenges at work and in everyday life seemed to fade into the background because nothing was more important or brought more satisfaction than *creating* your first child.

It was an exhausting time for both of us, but mostly for Kim. Our son was a beautiful and healthy baby, but he had an extreme case of colic during his first four months. As new parents, we struggled at times with how to handle our screaming baby late in the evenings, but our love and dedication pulled us through. We worked together as a team and our life had purpose and focus beyond anything we had experienced up to that point as a married couple. Despite the stress and challenges experienced as new parents, we'll always cherish the memories of this time of creation.

Becoming new parents is an example many of us can relate to, but we as creators are not meant to stop there. In order to experience the best life has to offer, we have to seek out ways in which we may become creators over and over again because, when we are creators, life takes on renewed importance and meaning. We become less worried about the future and disappointed with the past and more engaged with the present. Think about it. It's almost impossible to be disappointed, worried, or fearful when we're fully engaged in our work, a project, or a worthwhile hobby.[29]

Other than parenthood, where else can we realize our deep-seated need to be creators? Whether through work, outside interests, or hobbies, the options for creative endeavors are endless. For more than three years, I found that writing this book became my primary outlet for creativity, but I set other goals that supported creativity as well:

- Read six success books
- Plan each week on Sunday
- Read the New Testament
- Develop a detailed book outline

These goals helped hold me accountable to creativity and similar goal setting around creative activities can do the same for you. Instead of watching TV, I knew I had a more important calling. Rather than fume about a bad week at work, I focused my energy on creating the next section of the book. Remembering that "worry is the misuse of imagination," I channeled my thoughts, effort, and energy into writing, which was infinitely more fulfilling.

[29] The term "work" does not distinguish between work inside our outside the home.

Focused Engagement

Opportunities to be a creator are limited only by our imaginations, but they all have one thing in common—*focused engagement*.

Wouldn't it be great if we had jobs in which we felt this level of engagement? Some do, but the vast majority of us are in jobs or careers where focused engagement takes a great deal of effort to achieve. Many of us are not working in a vocation that is totally in sync with our guiding principles or considered our life's work. Even if we feel deeply that we are in the right position at work or at home, it's difficult to maintain a sense of wonder, engagement, and fulfillment with our jobs. We may enjoy the stability, but the actual work can become mundane and boring.

I remember the ads for Dunkin' Donuts in the 1980s where the owner of the shop wakes up early every morning with the catchphrase, "Time to make the donuts!" By the fifth morning, he isn't as enthusiastic as he used to be about making those donuts. We all have these moments in our job or with life in general when the alarm goes off and it's "time to make the donuts," but we do not want to make the donuts that morning. Because it's natural for us to be creators, we become bored with the same thing, day in and day out. This is when we must proactively change the way we approach the job or find an outlet outside of work to satisfy our need to be creators.

In this chapter we'll explore ways in which we can open the doors to creativity in our lives. In so doing, we'll gain more meaning and fulfillment in life. When we pursue creative activities in sync with our guiding principles, we develop a renewed sense of wonder, focus, and purpose. The mundane annoyances and distractions of life become less important.

As we explore ways to become systematic creators, we must be realistic about the numerous impediments to creativity—most of which are self-imposed. Also, we must take a fresh look at how we spend our time each day and be honest with ourselves when our first inclination may be to throw up our hands and say, "I don't have time for this." If we take an honest appraisal of how we spend our day, we'll discover that we do indeed have time to insert creativity time into our lives. We only have to exercise the muscle of discipline, which is what this book is all about.

Obstacles to Creation

Technology in the twenty-first century continues to expand our ability to do more things in less time. Why is it then we're struggling more than ever to carve out the time to do those things that matter most? Why should shopping, communicating, and doing our jobs take more time instead of less? Technology has blurred the lines between work and home, shopping and surfing the Internet, and communicating and texting. Like a dog chewing a bone, we have become addicted to these time wasters and need to do something to free ourselves from them.

Before we start as creators, we must be aware of the noise and distraction that conspire to derail our best efforts. These "surrogates" for creativity are subtle yet destructive by their insidious nature. Awareness is the key. Once we become aware of how we spend our time, we will be much better positioned to make the changes needed to accomplish all that our creative will intends. Here's a list of what I consider the primary sources of distraction that we must discipline ourselves either to either enjoy in moderation or to eliminate them entirely from our lives:

- Buying things
- Watching TV
- Surfing the Internet
- Playing video games
- Texting, talking, and all things "smart phone"

There's nothing inherently wrong with any of these activities; we all spend varying amounts of time doing them. At the same time, however, these are the areas in which we can spend countless hours, almost unconsciously. As we do, we become lost in the activity, and if we aren't careful, we'll lose many hours to a pursuit with little value.

In the Bondage of Debt chapter, we covered the psychological and financial implications of buying things, but there's another reason for its destructive nature: time. Shopping is a huge time waster and technology has not necessarily improved our efficiency. We now spend an extraordinary amount of time shopping on the computer. We compare features and prices, or fantasize about the next car or smart phone we want to buy. We'll often combine this pre-shopping research with time in actual stores, trying on dresses, shoes, and looking for that just-right item.

I can't stand the actual shopping process, but I spend an extraordinary amount of time shopping online. There's so much information, I find myself spending more time than I otherwise might have because I don't want to spend too much or buy the wrong product. But when does this research become an addiction? Am I really just "researching," or am I daydreaming about the various products or services and wasting time?

The Internet is an incredible tool. It helps us efficiently compare products, vendors, and prices. However, it can be a very big time waster as we spend hours searching and exploring. The same can be said for television. Although watching TV can be a form of relaxation, it can become our primary "hobby." Of course, watching TV is no hobby at all; it's merely a distraction taking us away from our true hobbies or creative activities. Even hanging out with friends can become a big time waster if too much time is spent playing poker, watching sports, or shopping.

Convenience and Distraction

I took my son to the Atlanta Falcons football game last Sunday and we had a great time. The game was incredibly intense with playoff implications on the line. We were sitting behind a family of four and the kids were about five years older than my kids, so I found myself observing them and thinking about what it will be like to have high-school-age children. The mom and dad were really into the game, but both kids seemed distracted. I noticed that the son was texting on his phone. Not just a few times during the game, but between almost every play! His sister was similarly distracted with her own texting habit.

Now, this was a game where every play was crucial. The Falcons ended up winning in overtime, but the whole time both kids were attempting to observe, cheer, and text (not necessarily in that order). At first I was amazed at how completely they had mastered the ability to text, and then I found myself stunned by the sheer volume of messages they were sending. I couldn't help but think they were missing out on a truly memorable experience. Why? For what purpose? Is this communicating?

The reality of being a teenager isn't lost on me. At that age I spent considerable hours in similar time-wasting pursuits such as talking on the phone or just hanging out with friends. These activities are just part of growing up. However, this texting provides a glimpse into the future of communication and the distractions technology will continue to bring into our lives. The conveniences are real, but we'll continue to find it difficult to balance them with the inevitable distractions.

Carving Out Time

I developed strategies for dealing with life's inevitable disruptions and distractions. The common theme of each strategy is taking responsibility and control of my day. I cannot overemphasize how important personal responsibility is here. It's up to us to eliminate the excuse, "I don't have time." We all make time for those things most important to us. Each of us is capable of achieving great things, but goals must be scheduled into our day or they become merely dreams never to be accomplished. The following strategies helped me immensely in carving out time for my goals and guiding principles.

Carpe Diem:

Commonly translated as "seize the day," this Latin expression should be our mantra for how we spend our time each day and each week. Seizing the day is about controlling our attitudes about how we spend time. It's about controlling the day in ways that give us time to pursue those activities that allow for creation. Control enhances our self-concept and confidence. We're more at ease when we're living a life with a plan. Therefore, we must begin by seizing today, not tomorrow or next week. The place to start is by listing our guiding principles and goals as we discussed in Chapter Two. This process will take time, but when done correctly, will surface many hobbies, activities, and even vocations that we may have repressed for a long time.

You'll be able to eliminate some television and Internet surfing and insert time to work on goal setting and accomplishing. Remember to break up big goals into to several smaller parts so that the goal doesn't seem too daunting. That was the only way I could read the Bible or write a book; otherwise, I would have looked up to the summit of the mountain each of these goals represented and I would have put it off.

What's your mountain? Each of us can climb the mountain and enjoy the vistas along the way by setting and achieving smaller goals and milestones. You will find that your days are much more fulfilling when a part of each day and week is spent achieving goals rather than just getting through work. I call this principle "building mountains out of milestones," rather than our more common approach, which is "making mountains out of molehills."

Build mountains out of milestones rather than making mountains out of molehills.

A carpe diem mindset will be difficult to achieve. There will be all kinds of roadblocks to developing this habit. Each day will bring many detours. It's easy to get swept up in the current emergency, but stick with the plan. If you get sidetracked for a day or even a week, don't get down. Set your schedule on Sunday for the coming week and prepare to get back on track. Keeping your goals and guiding principles in the forefront will inspire the discipline needed to make time for the most important life activities.

Time blocks:

The value of inserting blocks of time into your day should not be underestimated. Blocks of time allow us to be more effective. Multi-tasking is a misnomer. We can only complete one task at a time; therefore, it's vital to allow ourselves time blocks in which tasks or projects can be completed. One thing that really helped me was to begin each week by inserting blocks of time into my calendar. During these blocks, I ignore phone calls and e-mails, and ask for no interruptions. I try to make each block between one to one and a half hours. This is long enough to make progress on a project, but not so long that I can't be responsive to phone calls or e-mails.

This process isn't foolproof. Occasionally, I would be interrupted with last-minute meetings or emergencies, but whenever I made an effort to stay true to my time blocks, I was much more efficient and effective in my job. I followed the same process on the weekends. The weekends were when I allowed myself time to write. I found that getting my writing done early in the day was the only way I could ensure that it would get done. Once I completed my writing time, I was able to complete the remaining day's activities without any regret.

What about stay-at-home moms and dads? No problem. It's up to you to schedule time blocks during the day. What about using the time you have at lunch two or three days a week to serve as your time blocks? Communicate your plans to your spouse so he or she can understand and support your efforts to become more effective. Give yourself time to invest in one of your goals or hobbies. It really doesn't matter what kind of work you do, what matters is that you carve out blocks of time to invest in activities that allow you to work on your personal goals.

Regardless of whether or not you need a calendar for your job, I think keeping a calendar for your personal time is important. The calendar brings a timeline and accountability to goal setting and achieving—the building blocks of creation. Setting time aside and completing a task related to one of your goals really keeps the fire burning inside. I find time blocks to be islands in my week where I'm in control and investing in activities that are most important to me. It's a small habit, to be sure, but you will find that just as compound interest builds your savings, blocks of time spent on goals will compound into reaching milestones, goals, and dreams. I know of no better way to turn dreams into reality or interests into fulfilling hobbies.

Time wasters vs. downtime:

As Kim read this chapter, she called me out on this notion of time wasters. She thought some people might find my relentless pursuit of eliminating time wasters as an attack on downtime. She pointed out many of my own "time-wasting" behaviors such as watching Atlanta Braves baseball on TV, surfing the net for cars, or thumbing through catalogues and magazines when I get home from work. She's right. Just as one man's trash is another man's treasure, one man's time waster is another man's downtime.

One person's time waster is another person's downtime.

The top of the pyramid of effective living is balance, and I would be remiss in spending time discussing time wasters and roadblocks to creation without underscoring the importance of downtime. We all need time to just relax. We can argue about how we should spend this downtime—I think it's far better to read a book than watch TV—but each of us is different and my downtime may be completely different from yours. For example, I need quiet time by myself to feel a sense of renewal, but I have a colleague who is energized by spending downtime socializing with friends. What wears me out actually energizes him.

Downtime is for relaxation and renewal, both of which we need in addition to sleep in order to keep us fresh. The danger comes when we use the need for downtime as an excuse for not investing time in creation. If all we do is work (work that's not a creative outlet), watch TV, or surf the net, we aren't being true to our need to create. Consequently, we won't feel a sense of fulfillment in our lives. Downtime is a must, and none of us should feel guilty about our need to relax. As long as we insert time into our schedules to be creators, we'll find that we relish and enjoy our downtime even more.

Downtime without guilt is the best form of downtime of all!

Free the Creator Within

A "creator" is a person who creates; an originator. In order to become an "originator," we must explore our deepest, innermost desires and use the tools of creation discussed in earlier chapters such as experiential learning, guiding principles, and goal setting. The act of creation is the use of these tools to create something unique. Let me illustrate with an example.

My mom is an artist, and I'm blessed to have her original oil paintings throughout my house. She did not pursue her hobby as an artist in earnest until after her children grew up and left the house. However, her talent manifested itself in small ways early on, including copying cartoon characters such as Bambi or Woody Woodpecker into sketch-pads using charcoal pencils and colored chalk. As kids, we loved her sketches, but little did we suspect that the creative power inside her was so much greater than what was initially seen in these cartoon sketchbooks.

My mom was a very busy mother of three and had little time to devote to her hobby. Like most mothers, she really threw herself into her kids' lives without investing much time in her own goals and desires. Or, perhaps more accurately, being a good mother was such an important goal, she focused almost completely on it, crowding out other creative interests or goals, until her kids were grown.

After the kids left home, Mom found she had a great void in her life, as well as a significant amount of time on her hands. Developing her skill and experiencing life as an artist was one of her guiding principles, and there was nothing to hold her back now. She decided to throw herself into her art hobby by taking classes at the local college and experimenting with all forms of art media including sculpture, watercolor, and oil painting (experiential learning). She found that she had a passion for oil painting and she experimented on canvas, paper, ceramic tile, sandpaper, and slate (more experiential learning). Over the years, she developed several original styles in her artwork.

I use my mom's example as an artist because that's what many of us associate with the word "creator." When I hear people talk about creativity, I often think of artists and inventors such as Benjamin Franklin, Leonardo da Vinci, Henry Ford, and Alexander Graham Bell. However, it's important to consider the other ways in which creativity can manifest itself. In my own life, coaching baseball was a major breakthrough for manifesting creativity. As a coach, I found it very fulfilling to help kids improve as players, and to use the principles of baseball to teach everyday life lessons.

Coaching was an outlet for my guiding principle to coach, guide and encourage people, but I was initially fearful of the time commitment and effort it would take to be an effective coach. By taking the leap of faith into this new experience, I found an outlet for creativity that was very rewarding. In fact, my success in coaching was the beginning of the inspiration behind this book. Just as my mom was able to advance her art from sketches to original oil paintings, I wanted a chance to expand my coaching beyond little league and into the bigger game of life.

Think about how creativity can manifest itself into your life. What seed of greatness do you have inside that when freed-up and nourished could grow into an enormous talent?

Listen to Your Heart

So where do we start? What is that hobby, passion, or experience you've always wanted? Ultimately, the purpose of this book is to give you the tools needed to uncover these deep-seated desires and to provide strategies for incorporating them into your daily life. Listing your strengths, determining your guiding principles, and investing time in meditation and prayer are some of the key building blocks to self-discovery leading to creativity. However, it takes time and experiential learning to uncover and nourish these disciplines. Jesus said it best in Luke 11:9 (NIV), "Ask and it will be given to you; seek and you will find, knock and the door will be opened to you."

"Ask and it will be given to you, seek and you will find,
knock and the door will be opened to you."
– Luke 11:9 (NIV)

In the Amplified Version of the Bible, I find the very next verse to be extremely meaningful to those of us on this long and winding path to self-discovery. Jesus says, "For everyone who asks and *keeps on asking* receives; and he who seeks and *keeps on seeking* finds; and to him who knocks and *keeps on knocking*, the door shall be opened" (some italics added). Rarely is there an immediate answer given in these pursuits; rather, we learn during life's journey how we may take our guiding principles and make the most of our lives. Our responsibility is to continue along the path of creativity listening to our heart and pursuing our interests. We'll find guideposts along the way that will help keep us going when we hit those areas of resistance or roadblocks. When we hit a wall, we can't stop. That wall will have a door or window somewhere; we just have to keep looking and knocking.

My father, George Dupuy, is an excellent professor, passionate in the area of engaged learning, which is a method of teaching where the student learns a topic through case studies, group projects, and presentations to peers. Instead of memorizing facts and spitting them back on multiple choice tests, this method of learning is more akin to the types of problem-solving encountered in the real world.

Engaged learning is a type of experiential learning that brings the subject matter alive through real-world case studies and class dialogue. Although my father has used engaged learning tools for more than twenty years, this method has only recently become more accepted and recognized as a superior way to teach complicated material.

Based on my father's passion for engaged learning, as well as recognition of the lack of good text books to assist first-time job seekers in finding work, I co-authored my first book with my father. The title was *Career PREParation, A Transition Guide for Students*. The "PREP" in the title is an acronym for "Plan, Research, Education, and Perform," the four steps that will assist the reader in the transition to the world of work. Each section of the book is full of specific ideas, strategies, and exercises to help find that first job and get the reader off to a good start in the world of work.

I became involved as a co-author almost by accident. When I volunteered to help, I also told my dad I would draft a marketing plan to sell the book idea to a publisher. Dad later told me this was the catalyst he needed to take the next step to bring his dream to reality.

Unfortunately, my dad and I entered the world as first-time authors with some of the same limitations that we wrote about for first-time job seekers. Our lack of experience in working with our editor on a whole host of issues resulted in a less-than-satisfying experience. First, in order to have our book ready for sale in September, it needed to be in the hands of the sales people by March. We did not hit the March timing, and in retrospect I think it was strange that our editor really didn't seem concerned. Next, we found that the text itself did not fit neatly into the normal silos within the education field (e.g. math, history, or science). The editor was not able to help us effectively in this regard, so we really never found the right channel to create sponsorship within the company.

Finally, we did not have a strong advocate to help us navigate the byzantine structure of this large publishing house. As a result, the book became orphaned within the organization and the sales were dismal. The joy of seeing the book on Amazon.com was quickly replaced by the reality that we would not sell many books. My father and I were deeply disappointed and found our dream of becoming successful co-authors put on ice. The whole experience left me with a vague sense of incompletion.

I moved on with life and it was not until more than three years later that I reflected on what I'd gained from the experience and how I might build on it. First and foremost, I realized that I enjoyed the challenge of writing. It was a creative outlet and I found that the process gave a more profound meaning to my life. Helping others is a key guiding principle for me, and writing gave me a voice in that regard. Although I did not have the same passion for the "transition to work" subject as did my dad, I recognized that this book had the ability to make a difference for students in how they might effectively transition to the world of work.

What guideposts are you ignoring in your life? What passions, interests, or hobbies have you been stifling? Those passions, interests, or hobbies are the creative force in you longing to be unleashed. Unless you honor these deep-seated desires, you will feel a sense of lack in your daily life. Like a chronic backache you've learned to live with, you will forever carry a sense that you're not doing the things that, deep down inside, your spirit longs to do.

Lifelong Learning

Lifelong learning is taking your creative inclinations and putting some discipline and structure around them. In my mom's case, she took art courses and completely immersed herself in her art. She was fifty years old when she began this chapter in her life. Learning never stops. Just because you're on a career path does not mean you'll remain on that path your entire career.

As I write this book, thousands of people have lost their jobs and unemployment has hit a twenty-year high of over nine percent. As a banker, I'm in an industry that will be changed forever in the wake of the credit and housing bubble. Many will be forced into finding jobs in industries and with companies that they would not have imagined five years ago. Some will be taking a step back in terms of responsibility or compensation.

There's a very practical reason we should all remain committed to lifelong learning and creativity. Our core values, hobbies, and interests may become the foundation on which we can build our next career. Most career counselors and coaches agree that each of us will change jobs seven or eight times over a typical career. Rather than becoming reactive to this change, we should think within the context of our interests and guiding principles and become proactive participants in these changes.

I recently read about a dentist, Dr. Ira Wolfe, who found that he was much more interested in the small business aspects of his profession than he was working on the "drill and fill" aspects of the dental profession. He began by holding informal workshops for other small businesses on the key attributes of hiring good, reliable employees. His informal teachings grew into more formal articles and publications and before long he was conducting paid workshops for employers and employees. To fully transition from dentist to consultant and career coach, he decided to obtain an MBA.

Some might wonder why a dentist would ever change his vocation to that of a career coach or consultant. Dr. Wolfe says it's based on a very honest self-assessment: "The prestige of a professional job does not necessarily guarantee personal satisfaction."[30] Following our dream may mean less money or prestige but will likely lead to true satisfaction and achievement.

Work Toward Lifelong Goals

My father is fond of saying, "Life is full of trade-offs." Invariably, the quote comes when I'm talking to him about a challenge at work or a difficult life choice in which the pros and cons may not clearly indicate what direction to go. It's an inside joke between us because I groan so much when I hear him wax philosophical about life's big decisions.

Don't get me wrong; my dad has been a very helpful sounding board, advisor, and career coach for me over the years. I'm very fortunate in that respect. However, as I enter my forties, I realize the limitations of considering life's questions exclusively through trade-offs with no consideration of the heart or "gut feelings." The next job is

[30] Jo-Ann Greene, "Book explains why He's Working Harder but Happier", *Success Performance Solutions*, May 1, 2005.

chosen primarily by the next best opportunity to make money instead of working in a vocation that's connected to my guiding principles.

As we discussed earlier in the book, when the ego is central to our decisions, we tend to make choices that protect our ego rather than ones in keeping with our hearts. Life, indeed, is full of trade-offs, but we get ourselves into trouble when we choose with our head alone rather than in sync with our guiding principles, which ultimately come from the heart. Therefore, when you make a commitment to lifelong learning, consider your heart. When you discover your passion and pursue it, you'll find that lifelong learning is a joy that has the potential to lead you toward your true calling. You don't have to give up your day job in these pursuits, but you do have to open your heart to a more meaningful life.

Whether we're bankers, teachers, doctors, analysts, janitors, homemakers, or carpenters, we all question the ultimate value of our professions. Our job should never define who we are as a person. Those who define themselves by their jobs are missing the whole point of living a complete life.

Lifelong goals are those goals that expand our view of self. For instance, let's say that helping others is a guiding principle or lifelong goal that's important to you. But, you're very busy as an analyst for a large software firm. You travel. You have a spouse and two children who don't see enough of you as it is and you can't imagine adding another thing to the "to do" list. So you go through life working for the software firm, spending weekends running around with the family, and occasionally visiting with friends. But you're chronically unhappy with this life. You can't understand why because you have a wonderful family and a stable job. The problem is you're not investing any time with your guiding principles and you're out of M/S balance.

It's vital that you spend time with activities in keeping with your guiding principles. What if you took the following small steps toward meeting your goal of helping others:

Individual: Most large corporations have a volunteer program in which you could devote some amount of company time to help others. How about using your training to assist a charity with its computer system, or counseling students or adults on how to more effectively navigate their PCs? Now you're combining your passion with your training and expertise—and doing it on company time!

Family: What if you added the following goal to your list this year? Participate in one charitable event each quarter. Consider working as a family on a Habitat for Humanity house, serving meals at a soup kitchen, or volunteering at a local thrift store. You will make an impression on your children about the importance of giving back to the community.

Church: Ask your local church where you can plug in. Churches have many needs inside their walls as well as many outreaches into the community as well. Look for a service opportunity that matches your passion and skills with needs in the church or community.

You don't have to quit your job or give up your lifestyle to live in accordance with guiding principles. However, you have an obligation to invest in activities that allow for the pursuit of hobbies, guiding principles, and experimental learning. Such pursuits fulfill your God-given need to be creative; they will have a spirit-renewing effect on all parts of your life. If you don't invest time in these activities, you will slip into a rut and go through the motions. However, if you do invest time in your dreams and guiding principles, you'll experience a greater sense of fulfillment and peace in your life.

Family Adventures

I find that experiencing things through a child's eyes has the potential to reenergize our own creative spirit while encouraging their own journey of lifelong learning. Organizing a few family adventures each year takes everyone out of the daily routine and allows our creative spirits to shine through.

I remember the first time I took my son on one of these adventures. He was eight when I took him on a New York City business trip. We're both big Atlanta Braves fans and I was able to run down a pair of tickets to a Braves/Mets game and off we went to the Big Apple. All of the things I take for granted (and often find aggravating) about travel were new to him. He was excited about the underground train at Hartsfield-Jackson Airport, the plane, and the boarding process. The taxi into the city was perhaps the most adventurous part of the trip—seatbelts were a must!

We dropped off our bags at the hotel in Manhattan and I found that just watching him and pointing out various landmarks gave me a newfound excitement and appreciation for the trip that I had made so many times. My meeting was at Rockefeller Center and he was absolutely stunned by the grand scale of the buildings and the vast number of people. It was sensory overload for a young boy from the South, but he enthusiastically took it all in. The people I met with were very gracious with Jack and he was able to play video games in a separate meeting room while we conducted business. After our meeting, it was off to more adventures in the city.

Many of you reading this book would never even consider taking your kids on business trips. The only reason I started doing it was because my dad did the same with my sisters and me. Some of my fondest memories from childhood are when my dad and I went on teaching trips together. These were usually weekend trips in which Dad would teach graduate-level courses at Army and Air Force bases around the country. The highlight for me was meeting the pilots and other military personnel and getting the chance to see those incredible machines up close. I have vivid memories of these trips and they developed a special bond of love and trust between me and my dad. I know he had the same feeling about taking these trips with his kids as I do with mine.

Think about your own job situation. Do you have opportunities to take family on trips with you? It will take some effort on your part and calls to clients to explain why you're bringing your son or daughter along, but the adventure will be incredibly fulfilling for both of you.

Invest in Renewal

How many of you can't remember the last vacation you took by yourself or with your family? Far too many of us spend so much time working that we forget to invest time in vacations. I use the term "invest" purposely because a vacation is an investment in yourself and your family. We all go through seasons when we're so busy or our jobs are so demanding that we think taking a vacation is frivolous. This could not be further from the truth because the process of taking a vacation has a renewing effect on you and your family.

Renewal is important because when we get into a rut we lose our effectiveness. Many enlightened companies are beginning to understand the importance of renewal and have taken it a step further by adding the option of a paid sabbatical for their longtime employees. The majority of us will never experience a company sabbatical; however, we should all invest time in strategic vacation, so here are some guidelines.

First rule of renewal: get away.

My first rule of renewal is to *get away* from the mundane aspects of everyday life: school, work, homemaking. Getting away does not mean going on a luxury cruise or to an exotic beach; rather, getting away means changing the rules for a week and doing something out of the ordinary. In fact, there are so many things we can do that cost little to no money, but that can truly change our environment. By getting away, I find that I'm able to concentrate on my family in a way I can never do when caught up in the daily routine of life. Getting away allows me to appreciate all I have and enjoy time focused on the family. In today's world of Blackberrys and Wi-Fi it's difficult to completely get away from the pressures of work, but it's vital that we do so; otherwise, we've only taken the office with us.

I remember taking a kayak excursion off the Georgia coast during a recent family vacation. My wife and I had tandem kayaks. I was with our daughter, Danielle, and Kim was with our son, Jack. It was early in the morning and we were preparing to explore the marshes in the intercoastal waterway. The excursion was unique and exciting for us as we had never kayaked. The wildlife was abundant and a whole new world opened before our eyes with exotic birds, fish, and dolphins feeding in the marshlands.

The quiet, simple beauty of the moment allowed me to see my family and my life in a truly different and special way, as if we all were linked with the beauty and nature of the Creator. That three-hour trip gave me a sense of peace and connectedness that I had not experienced in a long time. I know of no better way to reconnect with family, nature, and God than by getting away from the pressures of everyday life.

Second rule of renewal: do something different.

The second rule of renewal is *do something different.* If your family goes to the same house near the same beach year after year, you may be in a vacation rut. Expand your definition of vacation beyond the beach!

What do you do on vacation? Where do you go? Have you fallen into the rut of going to the same place, with the same people, at the same time every year? This may make organizing the trip easier, but the vacation will lose its effectiveness for you and your family. Within the confines of how you and your family define a relaxing vacation, explore different alternatives. Think back to prior family vacations and use those memories to stimulate your thinking about where you might go and what you might do. Imagine unique family getaways and adventures like the following:

Camping: The purchase of a tent, gear, and supplies are a modest up-front cost, and the actual campground fees are much less than a hotel room. Activities including fishing, golfing, horse-back riding, and hiking. I love the peace and quiet of camping. For those of you saying, "camping's not for me," keep in mind that if I can do it, so can you. It's fun!

Church mission trips: I'm looking forward to going with the family on church mission trips when my kids are a few years older. Our church has mission trips planned to Jamaica, Costa Rica, and the Dominican Republic. It's a chance to see some of the most beautiful areas of the world while helping others by investing in their communities.

Explore the USA: The United States is as unique as the people that make up our population. Some of the areas I want to visit include: Niagara Falls, The Grand Canyon, Yosemite National Park, and Washington DC.

These are just some ideas that can transform a family vacation into s family adventure. Best of all, the options listed above don't necessarily cost a lot of money!

Creativity and Balance

What I've written about creativity should sound familiar. Creativity is an activity that allows us to become more in tune with our true selves. It's a doorway to better balance in our lives. Being in balance fosters a sense of peace and happiness that's impossible when our lives are out of balance. Creativity brings about a better chance for balance. Think of how one-dimensional we become when life is only about advancing our careers, making more money, and buying more things. Creativity can get us out of these ruts and break these cycles of boredom.

It's important to remember, however, that creativity isn't a substitute for balance. It's possible to have a single-minded creative pursuit in which all other activities, relationships, and responsibilities are ignored. This type of tunnel vision will have a negative impact as we tend to ignore warning signs that other areas of our lives are not receiving the proper attention. For example, I find that goal setting, action plans, and task lists (discipline) are extremely important for me to progress toward a creative pursuit or personal goal. But when I pursue these goals in a vacuum, ignoring the other areas of my life such as work, relationships, and renewal (personal responsibility), I get out of balance.

I probably struggle with this idea more than most. As I described earlier, I tend to be a grinder. I believe anything you want in life you have to work diligently to achieve it. When I create a personal goal, I put my head down and work hard to reach it. I may not be the fastest, the smartest, or the happiest, but I'm more determined than most, which allows me to work toward goal achievement with discipline and a grim determination.

The problem is that by keeping my head down during the journey, I forget to enjoy the incredible vistas along the way! I become so myopic about a certain goal, I reach it only to realize I really haven't changed and I really haven't enjoyed the ride. My creative pursuit has pulled me even further out of balance.

In my own experience, myopic behavior is driven by a fear of failure or that bad things will happen without my hands tightly grasping the steering wheel of life. Worry and fear become motivators. Setting and achieving goals is an important discipline, but when it comes at the expense of enjoying life's journey, we will never be able to truly find peace and enjoy life's abundance.

If you are like me, you must force yourself to stop and notice the beauty and miracle of life that surrounds you. Nurturing a feeling of enjoyment should start with the people we live, work, and play with. A feeling of gratitude regarding the many gifts that have been bestowed upon us will help us navigate the twists and turns that we inevitably face on the journey.

Emerson said that life is a journey, not a destination. Similarly, I believe that creation is a passion, not a goal.

Creation is a passion, not a goal.

To be truly creative, we must fight the urge to treat creativity as a means to an end. The act of creativity is the end in itself. Let me use an example to underscore this delicate balance. As I described earlier, my mom's art was noticed by others and she displayed her portraits, landscapes, and still-life paintings in local galleries and art shows, resulting in recognition by the art community. These successes resulted in commissions from friends, family, and others to do portraits. My mom began to see an opportunity for commercial success. She worked part-time at a Pier One retail store, but her creative talent might allow her to quit that job and do what she loved for a living. Little did she know how difficult and unsatisfying that transition would be.

Her portrait clients were picky and required a substantial amount of hand holding and reworking. She began to find that her creativity became a means to an end—making her customers happy rather than making herself happy as an artist. My mom is a pleaser, so she knocked herself out trying to please during the portrait process. Over time, she got burned out and lost the joy she had originally experienced in her creative pursuit as an artist.

For more than five years, my mom stepped away from the art world while continuing to work for Pier One. Only recently has she missed her creative outlet enough to start painting again, this time for herself. She has rented space in a commercial building catering to artists. She is rediscovering her passion for art and has a renewed excitement being around other artists. If she experiences some recognition and success this time, I think she'll take it in stride. She now knows the importance of art as her creative passion, and no longer as a commercial goal. She is grateful and her gratitude shines through her work.

Key Takeaways:

1 If you're not in a vocation that inspires your creative spirit, find a hobby that allows you to feed your creative desires.

2. Eliminate obstacles to creativity: buying things, television, surfing the Internet, and texting.

3. Build time blocks into your calendar for hobbies, education, and interests. Ultimately, you'll spend time on those things that are important to you. Claiming you don't have time is a poor excuse.

4. Your hobby or education may grow into a second, third, or fourth career.

5. Fulfillment comes from pursuing your guiding principles or goals. Even if you have a good job, family, and nice friends, you

will not feel peace apart from investing time in the creative endeavors closest to your heart.

6. Our jobs or roles should not define who we are as persons; they are merely what we do to make a living.

7. Invest time with your family doing creative activities. Family vacations can become family adventures that captivate the imagination of everyone involved.

8. The two rules of renewal are:
    a. get away from the daily routines of life,
    b. do something different.

9. At its best, creativity is an activity that helps keep you in balance; however, myopic pursuit of a creative endeavor may throw you out of balance.

10. Creation is a passion, not a goal. Creativity is not a means to an end, but an end in itself.

CONCLUSION

THE FOUR TOOLS OF DISCIPLINE:

- Delayed Gratification
- Personal Responsibility
- Dedication to the Truth
- Balance

When we become conscious of the power of these tools and how the successful mastery of one builds upon the next, we'll begin to see exciting changes. We'll gain confidence and will operate at a higher level of effectiveness. Most important, when we pair these tools with the attitudes of discovery and creativity, we won't just be living life effectively, but meaningfully—the ultimate goal of the Pyramid of Personal Power.

The Pyramid is a metaphor for life's journey and the self-discovery that results from that journey. The tools described in this book are only valuable to the extent we use them to further that discovery. The tools are not ends unto themselves. For example, personal responsibility allows us to be responsible for our lives—we refuse to be dependent on others for our happiness or our successes and failures. But if we stop at personal responsibility, what do we offer our fellow man?

If we're disciplined in setting and achieving goals, we do not necessarily experience peace, faith, or love. In fact, each of the tools of discipline is a means to an end. They are tools that allow us to strengthen our resolve to become better and to evolve as individuals. Ultimately, it's our fleeting attempts at balance in using our God-given talents to better the collective "I" rather than the individual "I" that result in fulfillment. Only at the top of the Pyramid do we begin to gain perspective on how the tools used to get there can assist us in maintaining a balance between discipline and love, personal responsibility and faith, creativity and grace, not just for ourselves, but for humankind as well.

Pulling these disciplines and ideas together into a cohesive whole is often a challenge. It's difficult to determine where we are on our journey—awareness of our strengths, guiding principles, and limitations are paramount for successfully navigating life's journey.

The Pyramid Journal

The Pyramid Journal helps to track our journey and provides tools and guideposts as we encounter life's inevitable challenges and roadblocks. It may serve as your life's guidebook and I have found it to be an excellent companion for the journey. It doesn't matter how you keep it—electronically or in a notebook—just taking time at least once a week to reflect on the key building blocks of your unique journey. Consider including the following topics/sections in your Pyramid Journal:

1. Strength and Gift Inventory: What do I and those close to me believe are my key strengths or gifts? What situations have I successfully used these strengths? Develop a strength and gift inventory in your Pyramid Journal. Exercise your strengths by incorporating them into your calendar. Focus on a key strength or gift for a month and evaluate how you were able to improve upon this gift.

2. Top 10 Goals: At the beginning of each year (or after reading this book), develop a list of key goals. These are goals that are highly important to your personal growth and development, but are rarely urgent in nature. They should be achievable, measurable, and in sync with your guiding principles. Frame these goals and keep them next to your bed, sink, or desk. It is important to remind yourself of these goals and provide rewards as you achieve a key milestone or goal.

3. Guiding Principles: Use the framework discussed in Chapter 4 to establish your guiding principles. These principles are meant to evolve over time, so it's important to treat your Guiding Principles as a living document using strengths and gifts to point you in the right direction as you face key life decisions. Implicitly, we know what is important to us, but writing it down brings a level of clarity and direction to our lives that is impossible to achieve without doing so.

4. Meditation and Thankful Prayer: Take time twice at least twice a day to meditate and pray. It's often helpful to write down affirmations and prayers in your journal that you can reference during this time. I take time just before bed and in the morning before the day begins to listen (meditate) and speak (pray) to God. This time is extremely helpful as a tool to relax before bed as well as get my day off to a good start. It's a good way to recalibrate my internal compass and get back to the core of who I am.

Although prayer and meditation have been immeasurably helpful in my journey, I've found that their effectiveness ebbs and flows. There are times when I'm under a great deal of stress and it's very difficult to quiet my mind for focused meditation and prayer. The only advice I would give during these stretches is not to give up! Rarely is effectiveness in any endeavor realized on a linear basis. We can go through long periods of minimal growth and then experience a big leap to the next level. The key to improvement is to consistently stay the course.

5. The Giving Habit: Resolve to be more giving with your time, talent, and treasure. Challenge yourself to give more each year in areas that are important to you and track your improvements in your Pyramid Journal. Whether it is giving food to homeless shelter, money to church, or investing your time with a charitable organization, we all are called to give. The more we give of ourselves and our treasure, the more fulfillment we get out of life. Through giving, we become more connected with our community, our neighbors, and I can think of no more important habit to develop. I believe you will find that whatever you give comes back to you in abundance!

6. A Spiritual Mindset: Take time each week to read and study the Bible. Whether through a Bible study group, Sunday school, or on your own, resolve to spend time reading and reflecting on the Scripture. I have found it helpful to reflect on impactful verses and write-out their meaning and application for my life. This practice made the Bible more alive in my life and allowed me to connect with the powerful wisdom held within the book. Finding the right translation and study Bible is important, so spend time in your local bookstore or on the internet researching the one that works best for you.

7. Creative Pursuit: Creativity is vital in order to maintain a sense of vitality and wonder in life. It's easy to fall into a rut at home or at work, so developing a hobby or creative pursuit is extremely important. Spend time in your journal brainstorming creative activities that are in keeping with your guiding principles. Resolve to incorporate these activities as goals in your annual goal-setting process and make time in your calendar to pursue them. You may find it challenging to incorporate these activities into your daily life, yet they are an important part of renewal and may even be an indicator of a full-time vocation later in life. Each of us is meant to be a creator, so claiming not to be "creative" is an unacceptable excuse and one that will limit your fulfillment and happiness.

The Pyramid Journal is a tangible way in which we may take the tools discussed in the book and apply them to our lives. It is a reminder and a resource to keep us on the right track and maintain positive momentum to the summit of the Pyramid of Personal Power. Each of us is on a unique journey and quest for effective living and I want to hear from you. Please send me an e-mail with your stories of overcoming obstacles, building success through failure, and summoning courage when the risks seem high by using the Four Tools of Discipline. Let's develop a community that supports each journey to the summit of the Pyramid!

David H. Dupuy
davidhdupuy@gmail.com

Printed in Great Britain
by Amazon.co.uk, Ltd.,
Marston Gate.